JOURNEY OF joy™

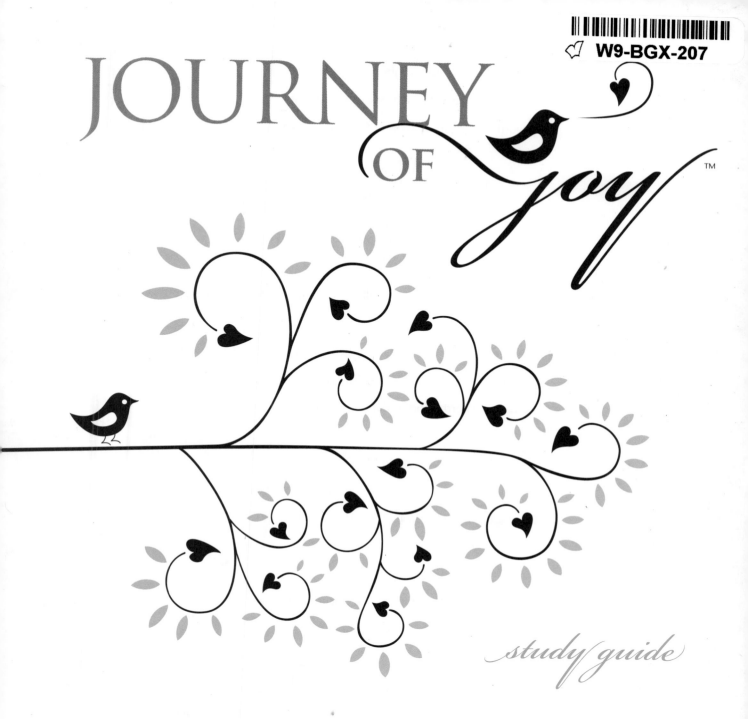

study guide

HEALTHY EMOTIONS & HOLY HEARTS™

11-WEEK DVD BIBLE STUDIES FOR WOMEN

CARLA GOBER

Executive Publisher and Producer: Carla Baker

Speaker: Carla Gober, Ph.D.

Lesson Authors: Kathy Goddard, Rebecca Timon

Contributors: Brenda Dickerson, Charlotte Pedersen McClure, Carla Baker

Consultant: Maria Ovando-Gibson, Ph.D.

Copy Editors: James Cavil and Randy Hall

Project Manager: Charlotte Pedersen McClure

Layout and Design: Ani Holdsworth

Illustration: Yiying Lu

Photo: Gordon N. Park, A.I.A.

TABLE OF CONTENTS

my

presence

will go with you.

I'll see the journey to the end.

EXODUS 33:14, *Message*

beginning this series...

Welcome to *Journey of Joy: Healthy Emotions and Holy Hearts.* Through this Bible study series, developed specifically for women, I hope you will encounter God in a new and more personal way. We designed these studies to reach deeply into the stories of people in the Bible—stories that explore what it means to follow God and experience healing that goes beyond personal brokenness. Some of the stories are about women, and some are about men. Some stories are about individuals, while others are about groups of people working together to understand God, as well as their own places in the world. They are not all success stories. Some are about profound loss and unfortunate mistakes. Others are about people who did not even profess to know God. While the people and stories differ, each one of them reveals something about God and about what happens when God's love touches a heart.

You will find that the lessons focus primarily on the main text and generally do not skip around in the Bible to texts that are unrelated. We do this in these Bible studies because we believe that the best way to understand a text or passage is to explore it carefully and mine it deeply until its wisdom and truth become more evident.

By extensively exploring a passage, we allow it to speak for itself. Bible study becomes a sort of conversation with the text—a conversation in which the reader and the text both play significant roles. Through this continued discussion with the text, the reader begins to "hear" the text speak in ways that a cursory reading would miss. Spending this kind of time with a text can be life-changing, because it gives a text the chance to reach into the heart and mind and affect the life.

This Study Guide makes use of various study tools, some of which may seem simple or ineffective until you use them. Drawing a text is one example. Many people declare that they "cannot draw," and so they bypass anything that has to do with drawing. We encourage you not to do this here. Drawing can be a very effective Bible study tool. Drawing a text gives you the opportunity to express how you view a text. This may sound strange, but you may verbally describe a text in one way and find that you describe it differently in your drawing. When you draw a text, you think differently about it. You think of symbols and meanings and the various components of the text. You will probably be surprised by how different your drawings are from others in your group. This is normal. While a text might be the same, it speaks differently to every person.

The studies use other tools to help in the study process, such as journaling and placing yourself as a character within the text, or various characters within the text, to try to understand what it would have been like to be each person. I encourage you to spend thoughtful time each week journaling in the designated places in the Study Guide. The Study Guide is much more than a workbook; it's a journal of your personal spiritual journey. You will find that the series is much more meaningful if you complete the Study Guide each week.

The lessons also encourage you to understand the historical setting, identify important words and their relation to the original language, and explore the text in relation to the texts around it. Is it poetry, narrative, a proverb? The genre or type of text often gives clues about its purpose.

A JOURNEY OF DEEPEST REFLECTION,

SATISFIED LONGINGS, AND LIVES FILLED WITH

MEANING,

NO MATTER WHAT THE CIRCUMSTANCE.

The main objective of these studies is that you will understand the profound sense in which you are loved by God, and that this understanding will affect your outlook on life, how you view others, and how you view yourself. To suggest that this understanding of God leads to "healthy emotions" is a tall order. We live in a world that is tough and often unforgiving. Our faults and mistakes loom over us as constant reminders of our inadequacies. We have learned to take pills for what ails us and to look for quick fixes. This is not a quick fix. A commitment to these studies and to the deep reflection that calls out to us from within its texts demands not only time but a commitment to new possibilities—and even change.

The journey of joy is not necessarily a journey of happiness, but it is a journey of deepest reflection, satisfied longings, and lives filled with meaning, no matter what the circumstance.

Carla

Carla Gober, Ph.D.

Introduction

ROADMAP FOR YOUR JOURNEY

OBJECTIVES

In this lesson you will

- Think about what prompted you to begin this journey.

- Discover God's imprint on you.

- Ponder the reality of God's plan for your life.

- Learn why God desires a relationship with you.

- Become familiar with the promise in the theme text.

ASSIGNMENT FOR THIS LESSON

1. Get acquainted with the format of each session and your personal Study Guide book.

2. Read the Scripture lessons, and write your responses on the pages in this first lesson.

3. Make a commitment to stay on the pathway for the duration of these 11 sessions.

4. As you begin Journal Your Journey, talk to God about your desires.

worship in the word

Luke 2:21-28, 36-38 ✦ Jesus Presented in the Temple

²¹On the eighth day, when it was time to circumcise him, he was named Jesus, the name the angel had given him before he had been conceived.

²²When the time of their purification according to the Law of Moses had been completed, Joseph and Mary took him to Jerusalem to present him to the Lord ²³(as it is written in the Law of the Lord, "Every firstborn male is to be consecrated to the Lord), ²⁴and to offer a sacrifice in keeping with what is said in the Law of the Lord: a "pair of doves or two young pigeons."

²⁵Now there was a man in Jerusalem called Simeon, who was righteous and devout. He was waiting for the consolation of Israel, and the Holy Spirit was upon him. ²⁶It had been revealed to him by the Holy Spirit that he would not die before he had seen the Lord's Christ. ²⁷Moved by the Spirit, he went into the temple courts. When the parents brought in the child Jesus to do for him what the custom of the Law required, ²⁸Simeon took him in his arms and praised God....

³⁶There was also a prophetess, Anna, the daughter of Phanuel, of the tribe of Asher. She was very old; she had lived with her husband seven years after her marriage, ³⁷and then was a widow until she was eighty-four. She never left the temple but worshiped night and day, fasting and praying. ³⁸Coming up to them at that very moment, she gave thanks to God and spoke about the child to all who were looking forward to the redemption of Jerusalem.

seeking through study

A dream comes true for an old woman

Anna was a very old woman when she witnessed the presentation of the infant Jesus to the Lord by His parents. From the court of women she watched the couple; they were obviously poor, as represented by not only their garments and demeanor, but by their offering, two pigeons. They held their Baby close as they made their way across the courts of the Temple toward a priest, who would perform the services of purification for the mother and the dedication of the 3-month-old boy, as the Law of Moses required.

She trembled with joy as she watched old Simeon, an aged priest of distinguished piety and reputation who had been assured by the Holy Spirit that he would not die before seeing the Messiah, come purposefully across the court and make straight for the young couple. Simeon reached out for the Baby, took Him in his arms, and eloquently praised God for showing to him the "consolation of Israel." Then he blessed the parents, too.

Anna came in close "at that very moment" and gave thanks to God. She told the good news to everyone who shared her hope and faith.

Anna, a woman of endurance

Not much is known about Anna except for the few clues given in three verses of the Gospel of Luke. And yet we can discover some of her story by looking into those hints.

Her name is the same as Hannah of the Old Testament, and it means "gracious." Anna lifted her praises to God for the child Jesus, just as Hannah had praised God for her child, Samuel.

Anna's father was Phanuel, a name meaning "the face or appearance of God." He was of the tribe of Asher—one of the so-called lost tribes.

Scripture says that she was a prophetess, like Miriam, Deborah, and Huldah in the Old Testament and the daughters of Philip in the New Testament. To *prophesy* means to proclaim a divine message, and to Anna was given knowledge of events as well as being one through whom God spoke to others. She must be included in that continuous list of prophets and prophetesses who proclaimed the coming of the Messiah. As she gazed on the little face of the Babe of Bethlehem, Anna knew that the past predictions of Him were fulfilled. Through her long, godly life her mind had absorbed the Old Testament prophecies concerning the coming Savior. Waiting unceasingly for Christ, she believed, along with Simeon, that Mary's first-born Son was the Messiah.

Her dream of the good life

Anna had dreamed of a very different life. Her faithful parents raised her to be a woman of God, to marry a good, righteous man, and to be a wise and fruitful mother. This was the hope of all young Jewish girls. When her husband died after only seven years of marriage, Anna was desolate, that is, alone, or solitary. As a widow she faced a long, lonely and cheerless life and a solitude made more acute because of the remembrance of happier days. When the earthly love she rejoiced in as a young, motherless wife was taken away, she did not place her hope in a grave. In her emptiness God gave her more of Himself, and she became devoted to Him year after year.

She had known terror. Anna was just a young woman when the arrogant Roman General Pompey rode his mighty horse into the most holy rooms of the Temple. She watched as 10,000 of her people and more than 1,000 priests were enslaved to follow the orders of the foreign ruler Herod for reconstruction and additions to the Temple to please his vanity. She watched and listened to the invasion of construction for more than 20 years.

"When death ravaged her own home, Anna turned from all legitimate concerns to join the band of holy women who devoted themselves to continual attendance at the 'night and day' services of the Temple. She was no occasional attender or dead member, but a constant, devout worshiper. Her seat in the Temple was always occupied."[1]

A shared life

Anna not only prayed and praised and observed people, she went out to proclaim her good news with others she must have known well. Scripture says she spoke to all "who were looking forward to the redemption of Jerusalem." She became a Christian missionary. "As she heard Simeon's praise for prophecy fulfilled, she went out to her godly intimates to declare the good tidings. Faith, through her long years of waiting, was rewarded, and she became the first female herald of the Incarnation to all who looked for the Redeemer in Jerusalem."[2]

mining the message

1. Although the Bible is brief about Anna, how many facts about her can you list?

----

2. List facts about your own life—your autobiography—that are important as they might relate to your relationship, or your desired relationship, with God.

----

3. Pretend that you can finish your story, or tell what the future holds if you continue your life as it is now. Be brief—just a sketch. Then in a new paragraph, briefly tell how you would like for your journey to continue. What does this tell us about your relationship with Jesus?

----

draw your story

Draw a picture of Anna when she meets Baby Jesus.

Did you draw joy on the faces of the old ones? What expressions are the faces of the Baby's parents? Do you feel a personal connection to Anna? Is there something in your heart that you would be uncomfortable putting into words, but that you could draw as part of a picture? What part of your picture seems most important? Why?

4. Did God have a plan for Anna's young life that included disappointment, death, unfulfilled desire for babies, loneliness? Explain.

----

5. Think about the words of David in Psalm 139.

Psalm 139:13-16 ✦ God, You Knew Me

13 For you created my inmost being;
        you knit me together in my
            mother's womb.
14 I praise you because I am
            fearfully and wonderfully made;
        your works are wonderful,
        I know that full well.
15 My frame was not hidden from you
        when I was made in the secret place.
    When I was woven together in the
            depths of the earth,
16   your eyes saw my unformed body.
    All the days ordained for me
        were written in your book
        before one of them came to be.

6. Think about this: What picture did God have drawn in His book before your birth parents even thought of you? Were your eyes dark brown or gray? Did He picture you with stick-straight hair or curly little ringlets? Was your frame to be tall or petite, angular or full-figured? Did He see you with a playful nature or introspectively serious? Open and gentle or intense and pushy? Self-absorbed or caring for the needs of others? A leader or a loyal second? Artistic or a mathematician? Melancholy or sanguine? Frightened or confident? A morning or a night person? Smelling the roses or just hurrying along? Believer or skeptic? God's woman or on your own? Spiritual or deeply God-seeking spiritual?

   Did you know that God had a picture book drawn about you and a written plan? Imagine what He created your inmost being to be like, and why you would praise Him for that. Are you experiencing the days that He ordained for you? Could you be confused about how the days of your journey that you have lived or are living fit with the plan written in His book?

   Discuss the paragraph above within your group. You are invited to discuss as little or as much as you like with others. Remember, nothing you say can be erased. On the other hand, much growth can come from sharing your thoughts and ideas with others.

7. Can you be assured that God knows and understands your anxieties and needs as well as your pleasure and joys? Read more of what David writes to God in Psalm 139.

Psalm 139:1-10 ✦ God, You Know Me

¹ O LORD, you have searched me
    and you know me.
² You know when I sit and when I rise;
    you perceive my thoughts from afar.
³ You discern my going out and
      my lying down;
    you are familiar with all my ways.
⁴ Before a word is on my tongue
    you know it completely, O LORD.
⁵ You hem me in—behind and before;
    you have laid your hand upon me.
⁶ Such knowledge is too wonderful for me,
    too lofty for me to attain.
⁷ Where can I go from your Spirit?
    Where can I flee from your presence?
⁸ If I go up to the heavens, you are there;
    if I make my bed in the depths,
      you are there.
⁹ If I rise on the wings of the dawn,
    if I settle on the far side of the sea,
¹⁰ even there your hand will guide me,
    your right hand will hold me fast.

8. The God who has a picture of you in His book and a written plan for your life promises to guide you with the same hand that crafted you. Do you have fears or thoughts that you may have gone too far or be in too deep for Him to "hold you fast"? Isaiah 59:1 says, "Surely the arm of the Lord is not too short to save, nor his ear too dull to hear." In your own words, tell what this Scripture means.

Write a word that describes each stage of your journey—past, present, future (one word for each).

Living the truth

While you may not share everything you have written in your Study Guide, it is important to complete it before coming to the group each week. Those who have not studied ahead of time often have the tendency to direct attention away from the text.

It is not always easy to take on another commitment and stay with it when your life is already busy and full. But with God's help you can do it! Make a pledge to yourself and to Him to commit at least three times a week for the next ten weeks to completing the lessons in this Study Guide. You will be blessed in countless ways when you make time to grow your relationship with Jesus Christ and grasp His powerful and healing grace to carry you through your journey to joy.

Lord Jesus, I trust You to "lead me in the way" (Psalm 139:24) as I spend time with You in studying and completing these lessons during each of the coming weeks.

_____   _____
SIGNATURE   DATE

integrate

Will it matter in the coming weeks, whether or not you are disciplined to study about the way God deals with people? How do you plan to personalize each Bible story to enhance your relationship with God?

_____

_____

_____

_____

_____

_____

SCRIPTURE PROMISE

God said,
*   "My presence will*
go with you.
*   I'll see the journey*
to the end."
EXODUS 33:14, *Message*

Turn to page 16 to

journal your journey

NOTES

[1] Herbert Lockyer, *All the Women of the Bible* (Grand Rapids: Zondervan Publishing House, 1961), p. 30.

[2] *Ibid.*, p. 161.

Journal your Journey

Search me, O God,
and know my heart;
Test me
and know my anxious thoughts.

PSALM 139:23

As you begin to write your Journal entries for the first time below in this personal Study Guide, use the words in Psalm 139:23 to get started. Be honest with God and with yourself. He created you with a plan for your journey. No matter where you are on that journey—even if you've taken a detour or two—write what is in your heart.

The ten lepers
OUTCASTS TAKE THE CURE

OBJECTIVES

In this lesson you will

- Examine the stories of ten lepers who seek healing by Jesus.

- Compare the need for healing of the lepers with the healing of a woman with long-term illness.

- Discover the concept of real healing as seen in a thankful leper and healed woman.

- Ponder whether or not you need emotional or spiritual healing.

- Ask yourself why you do not want to settle for ordinary healing in your life.

ASSIGNMENT FOR THIS LESSON

1. Read the Scripture stories.

2. Complete the worksheets for this lesson.

3. Sit in a comfortable, relaxed, and private place to write in the Journal Your Journey page. Take time to reflect and talk to God about your feelings.

4. Remember your pledge to work on this lesson each day in the coming week.

5. Reflect on what you desire God to do in you.

worship in the word

Luke 17:11-19 ✦ Ten Healed of Leprosy

[11]Now on his way to Jerusalem, Jesus traveled along the border between Samaria and Galilee. [12]As he was going into a village, ten men who had leprosy met him. They stood at a distance [13]and called out in a loud voice, "Jesus, Master, have pity on us!"

[14]When he saw them, he said, "Go, show yourselves to the priests." And as they went, they were cleansed.

[15]One of them, when he saw he was healed, came back, praising God in a loud voice. [16]He threw himself at Jesus' feet and thanked him—and he was a Samaritan.

[17]Jesus asked, "Were not all ten cleansed? Where are the other nine? [18]Was no one found to return and give praise to God except this foreigner?" [19]Then he said to him, "Rise and go; your faith has made you well."

Luke 8:40-48 ✦ A Dead Girl and a Sick Woman

[40]Now when Jesus returned, a crowd welcomed him; for they were all expecting him. [41]Then a man named Jairus, a ruler of the synagogue, came and fell at Jesus' feet, pleading with him to come to his house [42]because his only daughter, a girl of about twelve, was dying.

As Jesus was on his way, the crowds almost crushed him. [43]And a woman was there who had been subject to bleeding for twelve years, but no one could heal her. [44]She came up behind him and touched the edge of his cloak, and immediately her bleeding stopped.

[45]"Who touched me?" Jesus asked.

When they all denied it, Peter said, "Master, the people are crowding and pressing against you."

[46]But Jesus said, "Someone touched me; I know that power has gone out from me."

[47]Then the woman, seeing that she could not go unnoticed, came trembling and fell at his feet. In the presence of all the people, she told why she had touched him and how she had been instantly healed. [48]Then he said to her, "Daughter, your faith has healed you. Go in peace."

seeking through study

Leprosy

Leprosy, one of the most feared diseases of ancient times, damaged and disfigured the body. The first symptom of leprosy is a whitish patch of skin that can remain unchanged or even disappear. In the most advanced stages of the disease, the patches spread across the body and thicken into hard swellings. Leprosy destroys nerve endings, and the stricken person cannot feel heat or pain. Because cuts and burns go unnoticed, injured areas become bloody pulps. Muscles in the hands and feet waste away, and eventually the bones decay. Leprosy can spread to others, but only after long and repeated exposure. Symptoms can lie dormant for years.[1] Today modern medicine can cure leprosy. In Bible times lepers usually died of other illnesses because of their weakened immune systems.

Uncleanness

According to the Law of Moses, a leper had to live outside the community. A leper was required to wear torn clothing, have unkempt hair, and cover the lower part of the face, including the lower lip (Leviticus 13:45). If healing occurred, a priestly examination and confirmation of being clean was mandated, just as required in other quarantines of ceremonial uncleanness. (See the first record of leprosy, Numbers 12:1-15, Miriam's story.)

The Hebrew word *tâmê'* (taw-may') means being unclean in the literal sense, but especially in the ceremonial and moral sense. At other times it means being unclean in the religious sense.[2] In this religious sense the law requires a leper to call out *"Tâmê'! Tâmê'!* [Unclean! Unclean!]" (Leviticus 13:45). This prevents healthy people from entering the space required to insulate the quarantined person.

The picture of death

The Bible is full of word pictures of humanity's spiritual condition and God's restorative work, called redemption. We see in literally casting lepers out of society the symbolic treatment of sin. We are constantly reminded that God has no evil in Him, and His goodness cannot live with corruption and decay.

Leprosy has been called "a dreadful parable of death."[3] Lepers are treated as though dead and must live a living death in isolation. This visually tells the story of the effect of rebellion against God's will. It demonstrates the consequences of losing fellowship in the city of God.

To a much lesser degree of uncleanness and separation, women were ceremonially unclean for seven days from the beginning of monthly menstruation. The woman of Luke 8, who has been hemorrhaging for twelve years, is as unclean as the lepers, although she may be living as an untouchable in the back of her own home. More likely her father cast her out or her husband divorced her.

She is destitute, having spent all her money, perhaps her dowry, to find a cure, but no one she consults can stop the flow. Her constant state of bleeding "represents the ever-flowing fountain of sin,"[4] but humanity cannot find an adequate human tourniquet to stop the flow of rebellion bubbling up from the heart. A Greater Physician must staunch the flow.

We're in this together

Being a leper built up social barriers, but it also broke down religious, national, and ethnic barriers. The ten lepers stand together calling in unison. They recognize the authority of Jesus and call Him "Master." They make a concerted effort to attract His attention. They call loudly, begging Him simply to have mercy on them. "In the common tragedy of their leprosy they had forgotten they were Jews and Samaritans and remembered only that they were men in need."[5]

To see and to *SEE*

Jesus saw the lepers. The Greek word *ĕidō* (i´-do) means to see (literally or figuratively) by implication, to know, to perceive, to know intimately. *The Message:*

The Bible in Contemporary English, translated by Eugene Peterson, catches this deeper connotation: "Taking a good look at them, he said, 'Go show yourselves to the priests.'"

When Jesus sees the lepers, when He pauses to turn and take a good look at them, when He peers deeply into their souls, He *SEES* them. He sees them as they had been long before the white scaly disease ravaged their bodies, eating fingers and noses; not as now, wearing dirty, torn clothes with unkempt hair. He sees them also as they will become: medically and ceremonially healed and restored to their homes, socially healed and restored to their families and villages, and spiritually restored to their right to worship and fellowship in the synagogue.

Indeed, Jesus *SEES* the lepers so clearly that He instructs them to go show themselves to the priest to be inspected and pronounced clean. Jesus is not seeing the outward appearance of foul disease—He is looking at the heart's desire for mercy and restoration. He *SEES* the lepers in a state of wellness—even before He heals them.

To touch and to *TOUCH*

The woman pushes into the crowd as it presses in close to Jesus, who is making His way slowly through town. This ill, unnamed, desperate outcast woman reaches anonymously from behind. She's heard that Jesus does marvelous things. Perhaps His prayers will intercede for her if she can just touch the edge of His prayer shawl, where the blue tassels hang from the ends. This is her last attempt to find relief. Finally she finds the space to lower herself into a bowing posture and wriggles between the press of flesh to touch the hem of His garment.

"With the eye of His spirit"[6] Jesus can *SEE* the heart of the woman. He asks, "Who *TOUCHED* me?" Of all the people that day who touched Jesus, this woman is the only one who is healed. She touches not only His tassels but also *TOUCHES* the heart of Jesus.

The leper cleansed

The Greek word *katharizō* (kath-ar-id´-zo) means to make clean (literally or figuratively), to purge, to purify.

To obey Jesus defies social custom and religious laws. The lepers begin their journey toward the priestly inspection point. Perhaps they have walked all the way into the midst of the town, which is precisely from where the law shuts them out. Somewhere along the way, ten lepers see their bodies purged of disease, their skin newly purified. In joy they continue with their mission.

One healed leper turns around and runs back to Jesus, where he throws himself down at the feet of the Master. This fellow is still ceremonially unclean and happens to be a Samaritan. An unclean Gentile touches this Jewish Rabbi. Scandalous! And he worships Jesus in health and gratitude.

A leper is made whole

The Greek word *sōzō* (sode´-zo) means to save (literally or figuratively), to deliver, to preserve. The King James Version of the Bible translates it as "made whole."

Jesus is astonished to see that a Gentile, not a Jew, *SEES* Him for who He really is—the Son of God, the promised Messiah. Now Jesus is free to complete the healing process, to save him from spiritual death. He spiritually cleanses the man and saves him from his sins by stating, "You are made whole." The former leper is now free to joyfully pursue a life of physical and emotional health with spiritual wholeness.

The woman is made whole

No strange, mystical force oozes out of Jesus of Nazareth, unintentionally healing everyone He happens to touch. It is impossible for Jesus not to know who touches Him, because He knows everything. He allows this to happen.

Jesus calls out like a parent, "Who touched me? What have you done?" He gives opportunity for her to own up to her action. This is not to make her feel helpless, but to feel helped. He wants her to feel inadequate only that she might *SEE* that it is not magical but divine power that stops the slow drain of death and restores life. He wants her to desire more than to be made well. He wants her to desire to be made whole.

The town knows her as an untouchable. When Jesus pronounces her clean and touchable, He restores her to society. Although her medical condition is not the result of any sins she may have committed, Jesus demonstrates that she is healed from her *SIN* (which leads to eternal death) by reversing the life-draining flow of her blood and taking it upon Himself. Soon, through the shedding of His blood, He will stop the life-draining effects of *SIN* and symbolically reinstate all human-kind back into the garden. The life-draining flow becomes the life-giving flow.

mining the message

1. Read Leviticus 13:45, 46. How would these restrictions impact every aspect of a person's life? Do you think the restrictions were fair? In ancient times people believed in the "finger of God"—that all calamity was a direct result of God punishing the sinner. How would this concept increase a leper's suffering?

draw your story

Draw a picture of the scene from Luke 17:11-19 or from 8:40-48. Use crayons or markers to create plenty of color.

Are the colors in the scene dark or bright, subdued or energetic? Are the faces sad or happy, pained or relieved? If your picture were audible, would the sounds be loud or muted, clear or muddled? What does your drawing reveal about how you feel about your life at present?

2. Why do you think Jesus required the lepers to do something rather than healing them on the spot? (See 2 Kings 5:10-15, the leper Naaman's story.)

----

3. Only one leper returns to Jesus, opening the way to receive something more. What does he receive from Jesus that the other nine missed?

----

4. Why did Jesus call the one cleansed leper who returns a "foreigner"? Was He being insensitive?

----

5. Do you think the leper was able to SEE that he didn't need to go to the priest to be pronounced clean? Who is his priest?

----

6. Compare and contrast the healing of the woman with the healing of the ten lepers. In what ways are their situations similar or dissimilar? Describe the process of healing for each.

----

7. Why is it important for the woman to come forward rather than leave unnoticed?

Reflection story

Lydia opened her eyes and looked at her alarm clock. *Yea!* she thought. Waking several minutes before her alarm rang gave her extra time to prepare for her day—her *big* day. Before hopping into the shower, she glanced at herself in the mirror. "Yikes! What's this?" she asked herself, touching a red swollen bump on her cheek. "No. Not today," she moaned.

Knowing that high-stress times in her life usually caused outbreaks of acne, she scolded herself for not buying Acne Be Gone, the miracle cure advertised on the Home Shopping Network. She determined to buy it, but that wouldn't help her now. Today she would make her first solo project proposal to the inner circle of administrators. This presentation could change her life. She—Lydia Martina Smyth—was poised to move up the corporate ladder.

By the time she stood before the executives to make her pitch, the bump had friends. A concealer stick had helped, and she managed to forget her appearance in the excitement of the moment. She nailed the proposal presentation, and her boss, clearly impressed, said, "We'll let you know our decision in 48 hours." Lydia was ecstatic.

The next morning the bumps had spread to the other cheek. She noticed that none of them had formed the white pustules common to acne. "What's going on?" she wondered, but the good news her boss had for her the next day pushed all worries about a case of "teenage acne" out of her thirty-something brain. She was "movin' up."

Organizing a new office and recruiting a cadre of coworkers for the project consumed all her waking hours. She didn't have time to worry about the bumps taking over her face. Nothing she bought at the local pharmacy had slowed their multiplication, but they would have to wait. Eventually Lydia found time to call her doctor and get a referral to see a dermatologist.

"I have bad news, Lydia," the dermatologist said. "The outbreak on your skin isn't acne, a rash, or an allergy. It's a reaction to what's going on inside your body. I think you have a rare form of cancer. We'll need to run a series of tests to make sure."

Four words—*rare form of cancer*—and Lydia's life made a seismic shift. Gone were thoughts for the project of a lifetime. A new "project" had taken center stage.

Reflect

Have you or a loved one experienced a crisis that caused your world to become focused so completely on the crisis that it was impossible for you to experience a life of normal activities, hopes, and dreams? Can you relate to someone whose life seems hopeless?

Living the truth

On a scale of 1-10, with 10 being the best place to be, place a large dot (●) on the line that indicates at what point your physical problems (headache, pain, aches, disability) affect your daily sense of well-being. Use a check mark (✓) to indicate where your negative emotions (sadness, worry, anxiety, feelings of being wounded, need for affirmation or encouragement) affect you daily.

1 _____ 10
    2   3   4   5   6   7   8   9

Will you demonstrate to God that you believe He will heal your emotional needs and fill your spiritual longing? How?

integrate

Imagine the changed lives of the ten lepers after Jesus healed them and how His healing power and compassion reversed the life of the unclean woman. What has He done for you? Or what do you want Him to do for you?

Leave the space provided below for a special assignment from the Bible study leader after you have viewed the presentation for Session 2.

SCRIPTURE PROMISE

*Though your sins are
like scarlet,
They shall be white
as snow;
Though they are red
as crimson,
They shall be
like wool.*

ISAIAH 1:18

NOTES

[1] V. Gilbert Beers, *Prophecies and Miracles: The Work of Elijah and Elisha,* The Book of Life (Grand Rapids: Zondervan Corporation, 1980), vol. 13, p. 154.

[2] James Strong, *The New Strong's Exhaustive Concordance of the Bible* (Nashville: Thomas Nelson Publishers, 1990), p. 51.

[3] Richard C. Trench, *The Miracles and Parables of Christ* (USA: AMG Publishers, 1996), p. 142.

[4] *Ibid.,* p. 127.

[5] William Barclay, *The Gospel of Luke,* The Daily Bible Study Series, revised edition (Philadelphia: Westminster Press, 1975 revision), p. 217.

[6] Trench, p. 124.

journal your journey

Is there something more that Jesus is waiting to give to you? What keeps you from asking, from throwing yourself at His feet? What keeps you from reaching out to touch Him?

Folly and Wisdom
A Word to Be Wise

OBJECTIVES

In this lesson you will

- Learn the historical context of Wisdom Literature.

- Explore the Biblical meaning of Wisdom.

- Contrast Wisdom and Foolishness.

- Reflect on Wisdom's role in your life.

- Create your own picture words of Wisdom.

ASSIGNMENT FOR THIS LESSON

1. Read the Proverbs 7 and 8 accounts of Wisdom and Folly.

2. Keep in mind that the Scripture texts in this lesson use a poetic device called personification to depict an object or concept in human form. In this case the concepts of Wisdom and Folly are depicted as persons.

3. As you study, consider the contrast between choosing a wise or foolish course of action and its consequences,

4. During your journaling time, reflect and pray about areas of your life where you need wisdom now.

Proverbs 7:6-27 ✦ Warning Against the Adulteress

⁶ At the window of my house
    I looked out through the lattice.
⁷ I saw among the simple,
    I noticed among the young men,
    a youth who lacked judgment.
⁸ He was going down the street near
    her corner,
    walking along in the direction of
    her house
⁹ at twilight, as the day was fading,
    as the dark of night set in.
¹⁰ Then out came a woman to meet him,
    dressed like a prostitute and with
    crafty intent.
¹¹ (She is loud and defiant,
    her feet never stay at home;
¹² now in the street, now in the squares,
    at every corner she lurks.)
¹³ She took hold of him and kissed him
    and with a brazen face she said:
¹⁴ "I have fellowship offerings at home;
    today I fulfilled my vows.
¹⁵ So I came out to meet you;
    I looked for you and have found you!
¹⁶ I have covered my bed
    with colored linens from Egypt.
¹⁷ I have perfumed my bed
    with myrrh, aloes and cinnamon.
¹⁸ Come, let's drink deep of love till
    morning;
    let's enjoy ourselves with love!
¹⁹ My husband is not at home;
    he has gone on a long journey.
²⁰ He took his purse filled with money
    and will not be home till full moon."
²¹ With persuasive words she led

him astray;
    she seduced him with her
    smooth talk.
²² All at once he followed her
    like an ox going to the slaughter,
  like a deer stepping into a noose
²³   till an arrow pierces his liver,
  like a bird darting into a snare,
    little knowing it will cost him his life.
²⁴ Now then, my sons, listen to me;
    pay attention to what I say.
²⁵ Do not let your heart turn to her ways
    or stray into her paths.
²⁶ Many are the victims she has brought
    down;
    her slain are a mighty throng.
²⁷ Her house is a highway to the grave,
    leading down to the chambers
    of death.

Proverbs 8:1-36 ✦ Wisdom's Call

¹ Does not wisdom call out?
    Does not understanding raise
    her voice?
² On the heights along the way,
    where the paths meet, she
    takes her stand;
³ beside the gates leading into the city,
    at the entrances, she cries aloud:
⁴ "To you, O men, I call out;
    I raise my voice to all mankind.
⁵ You who are simple, gain prudence;
    you who are foolish, gain
    understanding.
⁶ Listen, for I have worthy things to say;
    I open my lips to speak what is right.
⁷ My mouth speaks what is true,
    for my lips detest wickedness.

folly

⁸All the words of my mouth are just;
    none of them is crooked or perverse.
⁹To the discerning all of them are right;
    they are faultless to those who
        have knowledge.
¹⁰Choose my instruction instead of silver,
    knowledge rather than choice gold,
¹¹for wisdom is more precious
        than rubies,
    and nothing you desire can
        compare with her.
¹²"I, wisdom, dwell together with
        prudence;
    I possess knowledge and
        discretion.
¹³To fear the LORD is to hate evil;
    I hate pride and arrogance,
    evil behavior and perverse speech.
¹⁴Counsel and sound judgment are mine;
    I have understanding and power.
¹⁵By me kings reign
    and rulers make laws that are just;
¹⁶by me princes govern,
    and all nobles who rule on earth.
¹⁷I love those who love me,
    and those who seek me find me.
¹⁸With me are riches and honor,
    enduring wealth and prosperity.
¹⁹My fruit is better than fine gold;
    what I yield surpasses choice silver.
²⁰I walk in the way of righteousness,
    along the paths of justice,
²¹bestowing wealth on those who
        love me
    and making their treasuries full.
²²The LORD brought me forth as the
        first of his works,
    before his deeds of old;
²³I was appointed from eternity,
    from the beginning, before the
        world began.

²⁴When there were no oceans, I
        was given birth,
    when there were no springs
        abounding with water;
²⁵before the mountains were
        settled in place,
    before the hills, I was given birth,
²⁶before he made the earth or its fields
    or any of the dust of the world.
²⁷I was there when he set the
        heavens in place,
    when he marked out the horizon
        on the face of the deep,
²⁸when he established the clouds above
    and fixed securely the
        fountains of the deep,
²⁹when he gave the sea its boundary
    so the waters would not
        overstep his command,
    and when he marked out the
        foundations of the earth.
³⁰Then I was the craftsman at his side.
    I was filled with delight day after day,
        rejoicing always in his presence,
³¹rejoicing in his whole world
    and delighting in mankind.
³²"Now then, my sons, listen to me;
    blessed are those who keep
        my ways.
³³Listen to my instruction and be wise;
    do not ignore it.
³⁴Blessed is the man who listens to me,
    watching daily at my doors,
    waiting at my doorway.
³⁵For whoever finds me finds life
    and receives favor from the LORD.
³⁶But whoever fails to find me
        harms himself;
    all who hate me love death."

3

wisdom

Wisdom literature

"The ancient Near East has yielded a great deal of what scholars call 'wisdom literature'—texts that instruct the reader about life, virtue and social interaction or reflect upon profound issues."[1]

In addition to Israel, other nations also had wisdom literature. One example from ancient Egypt includes *The Instruction of Vizier Prah-hotep,* from the Fifth Dynasty B.C., in which "an aged counselor instructs his son in how he should conduct his life."[2]

"It would be a mistake to treat the Biblical texts as just another version of ancient wisdom. In grandeur of scope, internal complexity and theological insights, the Biblical texts of Proverbs are in a class by themselves."[3]

Personification

Not just in Jewish Scripture, but also in other ancient cultures, Wisdom is portrayed as a woman. The Greeks gave the name Sophia to Wisdom. Scholars debate whether Wisdom speaking in Proverbs 8:12-31 is a characteristic of God, a holy attribute such as love and mercy, or a personality of God, such as the Word or the Spirit.

Two paths

The book of Proverbs contrasts two ways of life: the wise way and the foolish way. It uses the image of journeying along a path. The book is full of words "related to moving along that path: walking, running, following, stumbling, falling."[4] The reader is called to choose to follow one path or the other. The proverbs and instructions recorded here are verbal art, visually revealing in words the effects of choices made between the "contrasting paths" of wisdom and of folly, the paths of righteousness and of wickedness, the paths of life and of death.

In Proverbs, Wisdom and Folly are personified as women, each of whom seeks to persuade "simple" youths to follow her ways. Wisdom employs appeals and warnings, whereas Folly relies upon enticements. In these discourses the young man is depicted as being enticed to folly by men who exploited others (Proverbs 1:10-19) and by women who sought sexual pleasure outside the bond of marriage (Proverbs 5; 6:20-35; 7). In the culture of that day, these were the two most alluring temptations for young men.[5]

The woman of folly tells the young man she has fulfilled a vow, given a fellowship thank offering, and brought home her portion of the sacrifice. At first her words sound religious; she wants to share the joy of the fellowship meal, but unfortunately is home alone. Warmly personal, she's looked for the youth and found him. But sometimes the people who sound the most religious are the most seductively shrewd and dangerous.

1. The Hebrew word *pethîy* (translated as "simple") "implies an intentional avoidance of wisdom or knowledge rather than an inability to comprehend it"[6] and "generally denotes one without moral direction and inclined to evil."[7]

   How does the narrator of Proverbs 7 describe the young man?

   ---

2. What time is it when the story in Proverbs 7 begins? Where is the youth? What makes you think trouble is ahead?

   According to Proverbs 1:20-22, Wisdom is not at home wondering where her kids are. She pounds the pavement looking for the simple youth. She calls out for him like the town crier calling out to the city. She stands on a soapbox and shouts loudly to be heard above the noises of the street.

3. Read Proverbs 7:10-12. List the words used to describe the adulteress, the specific words she speaks, and the actions she takes. What do they reveal about her? What kind of joy does she promise (verse 18)?

   ---

4. Was this a chance meeting? How do you know? What do the words "All at once he followed her" (Proverbs 7:22) reveal about the young man?

   ---

5. The Hebrew word *'arum* (translated as "crafty intent" in Proverbs 7:10) means shrewd, which has positive aspects of prudence and cleverness or negative aspects of subtlety and cunning. How does the woman cunningly entice the naive youth?

----

6. How does the journey end? Was it full of joy? The young man's capture is described three ways. Which of the three trap comparisons (Proverbs 7:22, 23) is the most powerful to you and why?

----

7. Where is the house of the seductress? Who do you think is the most responsible for the "fall" of the young man: 1) the young man himself, 2) his companions, or 3) the woman? What might have prevented the outcome (Proverbs 7:4, 5)?

----

8. Refer to Proverbs 8 and make a list of the character traits of Wisdom that are affirmed and those that are warned against. Identify those you think are the most important and why.

----

9. Compare Proverbs 7:24-27 and 8:32-36. Make a chart that shows the contrasts between following after Folly and following after Wisdom.

Folly	Wisdom

10. If the narrator of Proverbs 7 and 8 were addressing a young woman instead of a young man, what counsels and warnings do you think would stay the same in the chart and which do you think would change?

_____

_____

_____

_____

11. Do you see images of Jesus in Proverbs 8? Make a list of these. Describe how following Jesus is the way of Wisdom.

_____

_____

_____

_____

draw your story

Summarize Proverbs 7 and 8 in one or two key sentences, then draw a picture of your view of Wisdom or a passage from the lesson texts that holds a special meaning for you.

Reflection story

"He's everything I've ever wanted."

"He's married."

"He's kind and generous and funny and smart and handsome. He's perfect."

"He's married."

"What makes you think you know anything about this? You're an old maid!"

That zinger hit the mark, but she wouldn't be silenced. "You're right. I'm an old maid. I met Mr. Right and let him get away. I'm a virgin, too. Did you know that? I've had flirtations, hopes, and dreams just as you have, and I'm still single. I may not know the ways of married life, but I do know you. I've watched you and cared for you since the first minutes of your life. And I'm a wise woman. I've learned life's lessons from living them myself and from watching the lives of others…like your mother.

"Listen to me. Please. Listen. If this guy does leave his wife and does marry you, do you really think you can build a strong marriage on a foundation of broken lives?"

"What do you mean? His wife doesn't love him, doesn't meet his needs."

"Oh, and she told you this?"

Silence.

"You think she won't be hurt, angry, vengeful? You think she'll just go silently into the night? You think his kids will like you and learn to love you?"

"He loves me."

"How do you know?"

"He tells me…all the time."

"How do you know he's not playing you?"

"He's not like that!"

"Right. A man who would betray his wife and leave his children is a good man. You're right."

Silence.

"IF he leaves his wife, IF he abandons his children…"

"Abandons his children…" For the first time she faltered. She hadn't heard from or seen her own father in 20 years.

"If you continue down this path, you will be the *other woman*, the *home-wrecker*, the *despised stepmother*, the *cause* of others' misery for the rest of their lives. All of this comes with the package. Romance and love, hearts and flowers, AND brokenness and hatred, resentment and revenge. Is this really what you want?"

The tears started and quickly turned into heavy sobs. Arms held her. The tiniest resolution began to take hold. A new path began to crystallize.

Reflect

Have you ever rationalized that a wrong course of action was really the right thing to do? How did it turn out?

Living the truth

On a scale of 1-10, with 10 being the best place to be, place a large dot (●) on the line that indicates the degree to which your actions and decision-making are influenced by the principles of wisdom found in the Word of God. Use a check mark (✓) to indicate the degree to which your actions and choices are influenced by your friends or the media ("what everyone else is doing").

1 _____ 10
    2   3   4   5   6   7   8   9

Do you desire the wisdom contained in all of God's Word to be your guide for living? What changes will you make to ensure that Wisdom is your constant guide and companion, and not Folly?

_____

_____

Carla Gober asserts that getting on a different path takes conscious effort. Leave the space provided below for a special assignment from the Bible study leader after you have viewed the sermon for Session 3, "A Word to Be Wise."

SCRIPTURE PROMISE

Show me the way
I should go,
for to you I lift up
my soul.

PSALM 143:8

_____

_____

_____

_____

_____

_____

_____

_____

NOTES

[1] *NIV Archaeological Study Bible* (Grand Rapids: Zondervan 1984), p. 960.

[2] *Ibid.*

[3] *Ibid.*

[4] Marcus J. Borg, *Reading the Bible Again for the First Time* (New York: HarperCollins Publishers, Inc., 2001), p. 149.

[5] *NIV Archaeological Study Bible*, p. 961.

[6] Kathleen A. Farmer, *Proverbs and Ecclesiastes: Who Knows What Is Good?* (Grand Rapids: William B. Eerdmans Publishing Company, 1991), p. 30.

[7] *NIV Archaeological Study Bible*, p. 961.

journal your journey

To which voice, Folly or Wisdom, do you think you have listened more often in your life? Where do you need wisdom in your life right now?

What hope or courage that can guide you do you find in these passages? Describe the path you are choosing to take you on your journey.

The woman at the well
BUCKET LIST ACCOMPLISHED

OBJECTIVES

In this lesson you will

- Examine the story of the woman at the well.
- Contrast this woman's behavior before and after she meets Jesus.
- Discover the two basic "revelations" in Christianity.
- Develop a definition of true worship.
- Reflect on the reality and depth of God's eternal love for you.

ASSIGNMENT FOR THIS LESSON

1. Read the Scripture story.
2. Complete the worksheets for this lesson.
3. As you Journal Your Journey, talk to God about His unconditional love for you.

John 4:1-42 ◆ Jesus Talks With a Samaritan Woman

[1]The Pharisees heard that Jesus was gaining and baptizing more disciples than John, [2]although in fact it was not Jesus who baptized, but his disciples. [3]When the Lord learned of this, he left Judea and went back once more to Galilee.

[4]Now he had to go through Samaria. [5]So he came to a town in Samaria called Sychar, near the plot of ground Jacob had given to his son Joseph. [6]Jacob's well was there, and Jesus, tired as he was from the journey, sat down by the well. It was about the sixth hour.

[7]When a Samaritan woman came to draw water, Jesus said to her, "Will you give me a drink?" [8](His disciples had gone into the town to buy food.)

[9]The Samaritan woman said to him, "You are a Jew and I am a Samaritan woman. How can you ask me for a drink?" (For Jews do not associate with Samaritans.)

[10]Jesus answered her, "If you knew the gift of God and who it is that asks you for a drink, you would have asked him and he would have given you living water."

[11]"Sir," the woman said, "you have nothing to draw with and the well is deep. Where can you get this living water? [12]Are you greater than our father Jacob, who gave us the well and drank from it himself, as did also his sons and his flocks and herds?"

[13]Jesus answered, "Everyone who drinks this water will be thirsty again, [14]but whoever drinks the water I give him will never thirst. Indeed, the water I give him will become in him a spring of water welling up to eternal life."

[15]The woman said to him, "Sir, give me this water so that I won't get thirsty and have to keep coming here to draw water."

[16]He told her, "Go, call your husband and come back."

[17]"I have no husband," she replied. Jesus said to her, "You are right when you say you have no husband. [18]The fact is, you have had five husbands, and the man you now have is not your husband. What you have just said is quite true."

[19]"Sir," the woman said, "I can see that you are a prophet. [20]Our fathers worshiped on this mountain, but you Jews claim that the place where we must worship is in Jerusalem."

[21]Jesus declared, "Believe me, woman, a time is coming when you will worship the Father neither on this mountain nor in Jerusalem. [22]You Samaritans worship what you do not know; we worship what we do know, for salvation is from the Jews. [23]Yet a time is coming and has now come when the true worshipers will worship the Father in spirit and truth, for they are the kind of worshipers the Father seeks. [24]God is spirit, and his worshipers must worship in spirit and in truth."

[25]The woman said, "I know that Messiah" (called Christ) "is coming. When he comes, he will explain everything to us."

[26]Then Jesus declared, "I who speak to you am he."

The Disciples Rejoin Jesus

[27]Just then his disciples returned and were surprised to find him talking with a woman. But no one asked, "What do you want?" or "Why are you talking with her?"

[28]Then, leaving her water jar, the woman went back to the town and said to the people, [29]"Come, see a man who told me everything I ever did. Could this be the Christ?" [30]They came out of the town and made their way toward him.

[31]Meanwhile his disciples urged him, "Rabbi, eat something."

³²But he said to them, "I have food to eat that you know nothing about."

³³Then his disciples said to each other, "Could someone have brought him food?"

³⁴"My food," said Jesus, "is to do the will of him who sent me and to finish his work. ³⁵Do you not say, 'Four months more and then the harvest'? I tell you, open your eyes and look at the fields! They are ripe for harvest. ³⁶Even now the reaper draws his wages, even now he harvests the crop for eternal life, so that the sower and the reaper may be glad together. ³⁷Thus the saying 'One sows and another reaps' is true. ³⁸I sent you to reap what you have not worked for. Others have done the hard work, and you have reaped the benefits of their labor."

Many Samaritans Believe

³⁹Many of the Samaritans from that town believed in him because of the woman's testimony, "He told me everything I ever did." ⁴⁰So when the Samaritans came to him, they urged him to stay with them, and he stayed two days. ⁴¹And because of his words many more became believers.

⁴²They said to the woman, "We no longer believe just because of what you said; now we have heard for ourselves, and we know that this man really is the Savior of the world."

seeking through study

Breaking barriers

A rabbi was not permitted to speak to a woman in public, not even to his wife or daughter. William Barclay describes a group of men who shut their eyes when they saw a woman on the street—and consequently walked into walls and buildings— as "the bruised and bleeding Pharisees."[1]

It wasn't just rabbis who did not publicly speak to women, but men in general. Most Jewish men of the time considered women and children substrata of society. The berakhah, a morning prayer of Jewish men, reveals just how low the strata was: "Lord, I thank You that I am not a Goy [Gentile], a slave, or a woman."

Separate kingdoms

The quarrel between the Samaritans and the Jews was more than 400 years old by the time Jesus sat at Jacob's well and spoke to a woman of ill repute in the noon-time heat. Samaritans were descendants of the northern ten tribes of Israel. Their capital city, Samaria, later gave its name to the region. Jews were descendants of the southern two tribes of Judah. Their capital city, Jerusalem, was rebuilt in the region later called Judea.

When the northern kingdom of Israel was destroyed by the invasions of the powerful Assyrians and most of the northern tribes carried off to other parts of the empire, colonizing Assyrians and other peoples moved into the ravaged region they called Samaria. Whether left in Samaria or scattered around the known world as the ten lost tribes, Israelites intermarried, combined their worship of God with pagan practices, and assimilated into idolatrous cultures.

Later the southern kingdom of Judah was carried off into Babylonian captivity, but they were allowed to stay together, and they maintained their racial and spiritual purity. When the Jews were released and returned from exile to rebuild the Temple in Jerusalem, the Samaritans offered their help. But the Jews did not consider Samaritans worthy to help with the rebuilding, and their offer was contemptuously rebuffed. Bitter Samaritans built a rival temple on Mount Gerizim.

Worship

Because they rejected all the books of the Old Testament except the writings of Moses in the Torah, the Samaritans had a limited knowledge of the coming Messiah. "Their main text regarding the Messiah was Deuteronomy 18:15-18, which says that He would be a prophet like Moses. From this they concluded that the Messiah would be a reformer who would teach them a better way of worship."[2] (See 1 Kings 12:28-33 for details of the first counterfeit worship system.)

Throwaway wife

Israelite law included a provision for divorce—initiated by the husband only. Marriages were dissolved contractually with a certificate of divorce (Deuteronomy 24:1). This divorce document most likely recorded a formula of repudiation declared orally before witnesses, such as: "She is not my wife, and I am not her husband" (Hosea 2:2). This declaration might have been accompanied by the act of removing the woman's outer garment as a sign of annulling the promise made at the time of the wedding to protect and provide for her.[3]

mining the message

1. Underline all the words in the Scripture text that relate to hunger or thirst. Draw a box around all the words that relate either to shame or living in openness. Circle all the words that relate to belief and being saved.

2. At the beginning of the story, the disciples head into town to buy food for lunch. The need to eat is characteristic of humanity (John 4:8). Where in this story do you see other aspects of the humanity of Jesus? Why is this significant?

3. How many barriers is Jesus breaking down by talking to this woman? What does this tell us about Jesus?

draw your story

Draw a picture of Jesus and the woman at the well.

How do you portray joy? What elements in your drawing are illustrations of symbolism? Are you surprised to see how many elements are associated with symbols? Did you draw something that you couldn't express in words? Which object stands out most to you? Why?

4. Imagine how the woman's body language changes when Jesus says, "Go, call your husband." Why do you think Jesus brings up this painful subject?

----

5. William Barclay writes, "There are two revelations in Christianity: the revelation of God and the revelation of ourselves."[4] Why is a revelation of herself necessary for this woman? Summarize the story using the idea of two revelations.

----

6. Imagine how you might feel after Jesus compels you to see yourself as you really are. Would you be convinced He can SEE into your heart? Would this be frightening or comforting? Would you want to hide from God or run to Him?

----

7. If God is spirit, God is not confined to *things,* and therefore idol worship is an insult to the very nature of God. If God is spirit, God is not confined to *places,* and therefore to limit the worship of God to Jerusalem or to any other spot is to set a limit to something that by its nature overpasses all limits.

   If God is spirit, a person's gifts to God must be gifts of the spirit. Animal sacrifices and human-made things become inadequate. The only gifts that befit the nature of God are gifts of the spirit—love, loyalty, obedience, devotion.[5]

   What reasons does the woman now have for bringing up the subject of worship? How would Jesus' discussion of "true worshipers" give this woman hope (John 4:21-24)?

8. What amazing revelation about Himself does Jesus make to the woman at the well (John 4:25, 26)? Why is this significant?

----

9. This woman goes from hiding her sad life story in shame and humiliation to broadcasting it to everyone in town (John 4:39-42). Explain why she can do this.

----

10. What two words does the woman say that invite inspection by the townspeople? Notice that when filled with Jesus, she reflects what Jesus says and does (see John 1:39).

-------------------------------   -------------------------------

Reflection story

Carmen swerved her car and screeched to a halt. She couldn't believe what she had just seen. The traffic behind honked her into the reality of a rear-end collision if she didn't get moving. The narrow road offered no shoulders. So Carmen drove into a gas station, turned around, and drove back over the winding road looking for the small dog.

Before she could reach it, the dog ran across the busy road in a confused state. Cars honked and swerved. Miraculously, it survived and came straight to her call, "Here, doggie, doggie."

She held the trembling animal on her lap and drove to a veterinarian's office nearby. She handed the dog to the receptionist and said, "I just saw someone throw this dog out of a car window. I don't think he's hurt. Please take care of him and find a good home for him."

Carmen returned to her car, climbed behind the wheel, and began to sob. A throwaway dog had triggered her deepest pain. She was a throwaway wife.

A rush of bitter memories flooded her: her husband's emotional and physical withdrawal, her suspicions and angry accusations, his denials and verbal abuse, the first meeting with the "other" woman, nights of listening to their son cry him-self to sleep, financial ruin.

"Father God," she prayed, "what can I do?"

The answer came: *Give yourself to Me, just as you are. I will never throw you away.*

Reflect

Where in this story of a broken and bruised woman is there hope for you? Do you believe God's words that He will never leave you?

Living the truth

When Jesus holds His mirror of revelation up to your life, what do you need to see about yourself? What do you need to see about Him?

----

integrate

What difference would it make in your life if you believed *fully and completely* that even though Jesus *fully and completely* knows the real you, He *fully and completely* loves you still?

Leave this space for a special assignment from the Bible study leader after you have viewed the presentation for Session 4, "Bucket List Accomplished."

_____

_____

_____

_____

_____

_____

_____

_____

SCRIPTURE PROMISE

With joy you will draw water from the wells of salvation.

ISAIAH 12:3

Turn to page 50 to

journal your journey

Turn to page 50 to

NOTES

[1] William Barclay, *The Gospel of John,* The Daily Bible Study Series, revised edition (Philadelphia: Westminster Press, 1975), vol. 1, p. 151.

[2] Jon Paulien, *John: the Beloved Gospel* (Nampa: Pacific Press Publishing Association, 2003), p. 40.

[3] Kenneth L. Barker et al, *NIV Archaeological Study Bible* (Grand Rapids: The Zondervan Corporation, 1985), p. 1548.

[4] Barclay, p. 156.

[5] *Ibid.,* p. 161.

Journal your Journey

Jesus sees our deepest, most vulnerable, most shameful places. Yet He says, "I love you still." Can you hear Jesus speaking those words directly to you? How does that make you feel? What is your response to such love?

Rahab

WHEN WALLS CAVE IN, MY HOUSE STILL STANDS

OBJECTIVES

In this lesson you will

- Examine the story of Rahab and the fall of Jericho.

- Compare Rahab's motives and actions with Joshua's.

- Contrast Rahab's explicit trust with the Israelites' lack of it at various times.

- Reflect on the deeper meaning of the scarlet cord in the window.

ASSIGNMENT FOR THIS LESSON

1. Read the Scripture story.

2. Complete the worksheets for this lesson.

3. Examine the significant role that trust plays in your life.

4. As you Journal Your Journey, talk to God about trusting Him and other people.

worship in the word

Joshua 2:1-24 ✦ Rahab and the Spies

[1]Then Joshua son of Nun secretly sent two spies from Shittim. "Go, look over the land," he said, "especially Jericho." So they went and entered the house of a prostitute named Rahab and stayed there.

[2]The king of Jericho was told, "Look! Some of the Israelites have come here tonight to spy out the land." [3]So the king of Jericho sent this message to Rahab: "Bring out the men who came to you and entered your house, because they have come to spy out the whole land."

[4]But the woman had taken the two men and hidden them. She said, "Yes, the men came to me, but I did not know where they had come from. [5]At dusk, when it was time to close the city gate, the men left. I don't know which way they went. Go after them quickly. You may catch up with them." [6](But she had taken them up to the roof and hidden them under the stalks of flax she had laid out on the roof.) [7]So the men set out in pursuit of the spies on the road that leads to the fords of the Jordan, and as soon as the pursuers had gone out, the gate was shut.

[8]Before the spies lay down for the night, she went up on the roof [9]and said to them, "I know that the Lord has given this land to you and that a great fear of you has fallen on us, so that all who live in this country are melting in fear because of you. [10]We have heard how the Lord dried up the water of the Red Sea for you when you came out of Egypt, and what you did to Sihon and Og, the two kings of the Amorites east of the Jordan, whom you completely destroyed. [11]When we heard of it, our hearts melted and everyone's courage failed because of you, for the Lord your God is God in heaven above and on the earth below. [12]Now then, please swear to me by the Lord that you will show kindness to my family, because I have shown kindness to you. Give me a sure sign [13]that you will spare the lives of my father and mother, my brothers and sisters, and all who belong to them, and that you will save us from death."

[14]"Our lives for your lives!" the men assured her. "If you don't tell what we are doing, we will treat you kindly and faithfully when the Lord gives us the land."

[15]So she let them down by a rope through the window, for the house she lived in was part of the city wall. [16]Now she had said to them, "Go to the hills so the pursuers will not find you. Hide yourselves there three days until they return, and then go on your way."

[17]The men said to her, "This oath you made us swear will not be binding on us [18]unless, when we enter the land, you have tied this scarlet cord in the window through which you let us down, and unless you have brought your father and mother, your brothers and all your family into your house. [19]If anyone goes outside your house into the street, his blood will be on his own head; we will not be responsible. As for anyone who is in the house with you, his blood will be on our head if a hand is laid on him. [20]But if you tell what we are doing, we will be released from the oath you made us swear."

[21]"Agreed," she replied. "Let it be as you say." So she sent them away and they departed. And she tied the scarlet cord in the window.

[22]When they left, they went into the hills and stayed there three days, until the pursuers had searched all along the road and returned without finding them. [23]Then the two men started back. They went down out of the hills, forded the river and came to Joshua son of Nun and told him everything that had happened to them. [24]They said to Joshua, "The Lord has surely given the whole land into our hands; all the people are melting in fear because of us."

²⁰When the trumpets sounded, the people shouted, and at the sound of the trumpet, when the people gave a loud shout, the wall collapsed; so every man charged straight in, and they took the city. ²¹They devoted the city to the LORD and destroyed with the sword every living thing in it—men and women, young and old, cattle, sheep and donkeys.

²²Joshua said to the two men who had spied out the land, "Go into the prostitute's house and bring her out and all who belong to her, in accordance with your oath to her." ²³So the young men who had done the spying went in and brought out Rahab, her father and mother and brothers and all who belonged to her. They brought out her entire family and put them in a place outside the camp of Israel.

²⁴Then they burned the whole city and everything in it, but they put the silver and gold and the articles of bronze and iron into the treasury of the Lord's house. ²⁵But Joshua spared Rahab the prostitute, with her family and all who belonged to her, because she hid the men Joshua had sent as spies to Jericho—and she lives among the Israelites to this day.

seeking through study

Setting the scene

Located five miles west of the Jordan River, Jericho's natural springs inside its walls made it an oasis[1] (thus the town's nickname, "City of Palms"). Tribal chieftains called kings ruled the cities of Canaan. The cities were not large by today's standards. The wall of Jericho was its security. "The ancient walls of Jericho were six and one-half feet thick and had towers of 30 feet tall in height."[2] Rahab's house was located in a casemate wall of the city—a space that separates two walls, the higher inner wall and the lower outer wall.

Harlot or innkeeper?

Scholars disagree on the meaning of the word used to depict Rahab's profession. Some believe the word describes a person who for a fee gives travelers a meal and place to sleep for the night (perhaps a little social entertainment also), and translate the word as *innkeeper*. Some believe the word describes a woman who for a fee gives a man a place to sleep with her for the night along with a little sexual entertainment, and translate the word as *harlot*. Some commentators even suggest Rahab was a temple prostitute in Canaanite cult worship. The Jewish historian Josephus calls her an innkeeper.

God Himself uses prostitution as a metaphor to describe the unfaithful nation of Israel forgetting their covenant with Him and running after other gods. Israel already played the harlot at Shittim (Numbers 25:1-3). They will play the harlot again when living in Canaan (Judges 2:17; first of many references in the Old Testament).

The two spies entered Canaan from Shittim. The story structure alerts us to expect the spies to continue playing the harlot; but instead they reverse the previous unfaithfulness of Israel and act as faithful witnesses. They enter the house of a harlot, but they aren't even tempted to play *with* the harlot. And rather than inviting them in for other enticements, Rahab invites them to listen to her testimony of faith in Yahweh.

The continued labeling of Rahab as a prostitute in the narrative is paradoxical because her only visible pagan prostitution is seen when she forsakes her Canaanite gods and chases after Yahweh. Yet she is labeled "prostitute" five times in the Bible (Joshua 2:1; 6:17, 25; Hebrews 11:31; James 2:25). Through this, God makes the unmistakable point that in His mercy He can turn shame into glory.

Flax stalks and a scarlet cord

Whether she is a prostitute or a reputable innkeeper, Rahab is intent on making a living for herself. Apparently she is a practical woman who develops another line of work. Clues in the passage suggest she is also a fabric maker. Flax stalks used to make linen textiles are drying on her roof. She also has handy a long scarlet cord; rope holds dye well, and pieces are cut off to throw in a dyeing vat.

When Rahab hangs the scarlet cord from her window, she and her family are covered with the mercy of a covenant. The spies have promised, "Our lives for your lives." They speak on behalf of the leader Joshua and pledge they won't kill anyone inside Rahab's house. Joshua saves Rahab and her family because she places her trust in the covenant oath and uses the scarlet cord as the sign of her allegiance.

Rahab reflects Joshua

Rahab's courage reflects the courage of her hero Joshua (see Joshua 1). She faces an unknown future with foreigners, but exhibits faith in the God of the Exodus, whose story reverberates down through the decades with such power that it melts the courage of pagan hearts in Jericho.

Although living in a heathen culture, she exhibits the behavior of a covenant believer and visually enacts Joshua's later proclamation "As for me and my household, we will serve the Lord" (Joshua 24:15). She shows as much strength of character as Joshua. "The corollary of declaring faith in the true God is 'put away foreign gods' and turn to him (Joshua 24:23)." [3]

Rahab responds to Yahweh

At the beginning of the narrative Rahab is in danger. She sees that the two men are from the house of God (this is not simply her ticket to freedom). She *believes* their personal God is greater than her gods. She *responds* by making a confession, by asking to be saved, by changing her lifestyle, and by working on behalf of God.

When Rahab affirms her knowledge of Yahweh and declares "I know" (Joshua 2:9), she uses the Hebrew word yâda' (yaw-dah´), meaning to know, to ascertain by seeing. Yet Rahab did not personally witness the mighty acts of God that she recounts. Actually, she probably knew very little about Yahweh. It was not the *amount* of her faith that mattered as much as the *object* of her faith.

The true Joshua

The angel Gabriel instructed Joseph to name the son to be born of Mary "Jesus," which is the Greek form of Joshua and means "the Lord saves." Jesus doesn't just save people physically, as did Joshua; He also saves people from sin. Those who are living with Jesus in His house when the walls cave in are marked as His own. But make no mistake: this mercy covenant is not a two-way covenant that pledges "spare a life, save a life." Jesus signs His covenant with His blood and swears, "My life for your life." The true Joshua gives His life to save your life.

draw your story

Draw a picture of the city of Jericho falling.

Is your picture from Rahab's vantage point or Joshua's? Are the walls around you or in front of you? In other words, is your viewpoint looking out of Jericho or into Jericho? Are the walls standing, or have they caved in? Or did you portray them both ways? Is the family in Rahab's house courageous or fearful? Did you draw a victorious soldier in your picture? Who is he? (See Joshua 5:13-15.)

mining the message

1. Make a table of lists: Rahab's *demonstrations* of faith, the *risks* she takes, and the *rewards* she gains.

Demonstrations of faith	Risks she takes	Rewards she gains

2. Why would staying in the house of a prostitute be a safe place for two foreign men?

----

3. What risks did the spies take in trusting Rahab? What gave them cause to trust her?

-----

4. What reasons did Rahab have to change her loyalty from her king and people to a foreign people?

-----

5. How do you know that Rahab had a God encounter prior to meeting these two men of Israel? Does she act like a new believer? (To help formulate your answer, write a list of clues from her confession of belief. How does she describe the Lord?)

-----

6. What does Rahab ask from these men and what do we know about her motives? What bargain do they negotiate with her? List the things the red cord symbolizes.

-----

7. Two groups of very different people reveal a total dependence upon God in this story—the Israelites led by Joshua, and Rahab with her family waiting in her home. In what ways is their dependence upon God similar? In what ways is it different?

----

8. Rahab lived in the margin of society in Jericho. When rescued, she was provided with a campsite on the margin of Israelite society (Joshua 6:23). Do you think she still felt like an outsider? How did she break out of the margin and become fully assimilated into Israel, so that the writer informs us, "She lives among the Israelites to this day" (verse 25)?

----

9. Read Matthew 1:5; Hebrews 11:31; and James 2:25. What do these verses tell us about Rahab? Why is it significant that Rahab "the prostitute" is an ancestor of Jesus?

Reflection story

Beka did not know how to pick men. Her three children each had a different father. The first one she had been smart enough not to marry. The next two she married, then divorced. She hadn't bothered to marry her current man, but took precautions to prevent another pregnancy.

"Blissfully happy," she said to herself and others about her current arrangement. But one day the carefully protected card tower blew away with an abrupt phone call from Human Services.

"We have your children in protective custody," the disembodied voice on the phone informed her. "We need you to meet with a social worker tomorrow."

Who would report her? And why? She imagined a dozen different scenarios. The meeting was tense. A teacher had discovered bruises on her little girl, her precious little girl. The boys had confirmed that her man was responsible. He hit them all—often.

How could I be so blind?

The caseworker was patient. When Beka finally let her defenses down, she admitted, "In my gut I knew he must be doing something to them. They were all afraid of him and worked hard to stay out of his way."

"Has he ever hit you?"

A knot cramped her stomach. How could she answer? If she said no, she would be lying. If she said yes, she would look really weak and stupid.

A small voice came out of her mouth. "Yes, he has."

"If you want your children back, you've got to get him out of your house."

"OK."

"Do you need help doing this?"

"Yes."

Where the courage had come from to want this, she had no idea. It was clearly outside of herself. She did know that life was better now. The kids' grades were up. Their teachers reported that they were happy in school. She had discovered that she could make it on her own.

If there was to be a next man in her life, he would not be one she chose. He would be a direct gift from God.

Reflect

Rahab had the courage to break away from her past. Her courage to act saved not only herself but also her entire family. What can you learn from Rahab's story that gives you courage to take action for the sake of yourself or those you love?

Living the truth

A metaphor uses a literal object to help us understand something less concrete. How does the scarlet cord in this ancient story help you to understand salvation?

integrate

Do you *know* the truth about God? Do you believe that truth will save you and your family? (It's one thing to believe and say, "Lord, Lord," but another to believe and respond.) Do you have the courage to make the changes needed to put you on the right path to the Promised Land?

Leave the space below for a special assignment from the Bible study leader after you have viewed the presentation for Session 5, "When Walls Cave In, My House Still Stands."

SCRIPTURE PROMISE

Give thanks to the
Lord,
for he is good.
His love endures
forever.

PSALM 136:1

NOTES

[1] *NIV Archaeological Study Bible* (Grand Rapids: Zondervan, 2005), p. 305.
[2] Ralph Gower, *The New Manners and Customs of Bible Times* (Chicago: Moody Press, 1987), p. 187.
[3] E. John Hamlin, *Inheriting the Land: A Commentary on Joshua,* International Theological Commentary (Grand Rapids:, Wm. Eerdmans Publishing Co., 1983), p. 19.

What contrasts or parallels do you see between you and Rahab, her family and yours, Jericho and the place where you live? Are you trusting Jesus to save you and your family the way Rahab trusted the spies and Joshua?

A sinful woman anoints Jesus

JOY: AN EXPENSIVE PERFUME

OBJECTIVES

In this lesson you will

- Examine the story of the woman who anointed Jesus' feet with perfume.

- Compare her actions with those of other women we have studied.

- Contrast the woman's attitudes and actions with those of Simon.

- Reflect on the true meaning of forgiveness.

- Ask yourself what you are giving to Jesus.

ASSIGNMENT FOR THIS LESSON

1. Read the Scripture story.

2. Write the main point of each passage in a sentence or phrase.

3. Complete the worksheets for this lesson.

4. Examine the role of forgiveness in your life.

5. As you Journal Your Journey, talk to God about what He wants you to give Him.

Luke 7:36-50 ✦ Jesus Anointed by a Sinful Woman

³⁶Now one of the Pharisees invited Jesus to have dinner with him, so he went to the Pharisee's house and reclined at the table. ³⁷When a woman who had lived a sinful life in that town learned that Jesus was eating at the Pharisee's house, she brought an alabaster jar of perfume, ³⁸and as she stood behind him at his feet weeping, she began to wet his feet with her tears. Then she wiped them with her hair, kissed them and poured perfume on them.

³⁹When the Pharisee who had invited him saw this, he said to himself, "If this man were a prophet, he would know who is touching him and what kind of woman she is—that she is a sinner."

⁴⁰Jesus answered him, "Simon, I have something to tell you."

"Tell me, teacher," he said.

⁴¹"Two men owed money to a certain moneylender. One owed him five hundred denarii and the other fifty. ⁴²Neither of them had the money to pay him back, so he canceled the debts of both. Now which of them will love him more?"

⁴³Simon replied, "I suppose the one who had the bigger debt canceled."

"You have judged correctly," Jesus said.

⁴⁴Then he turned toward the woman and said to Simon, "Do you see this woman? I came into your house. You did not give me any water for my feet, but she wet my feet with her tears and wiped them with her hair. ⁴⁵You did not give me a kiss, but this woman, from the time I entered, has not stopped kissing my feet. ⁴⁶You did not put oil on my head, but she has poured perfume on my feet. ⁴⁷Therefore, I tell you, her many sins have been forgiven—for she loved much. But he who has been forgiven little loves little."

⁴⁸Then Jesus said to her, "Your sins are forgiven."

⁴⁹The other guests began to say among themselves, "Who is this who even forgives sins?"

⁵⁰Jesus said to the woman, "Your faith has saved you; go in peace."

seeking through study

Banqueting

By the time of Jesus, the Jews had adopted the Roman custom of giving banquets and were enormously fond of social feasting.[1] Reclining at a table was the customary posture for eating a banquet. Guests rested on their left elbow and ate with their right hand. Most likely the meal at Simon's house was served in the home's enclosed courtyard, where the townspeople would have pressed in to find a spot to stand or sit on the ground.[2] Everyone wanted to listen to the local Pharisee dialogue with the amazing Rabbi.

Perfumes and oils

The *NIV Archaeological Study Bible* identifies four uses for perfumes and fragrant oils: 1) religious—the formula for incense and oils used for the Temple services was sacred and used only for the priests and Temple furniture; 2) hygienic—in pre-soap and pre-shampoo eras, oils were used for cleansing the hair and body; oil on the scalp killed head lice; 3) medicinal—oils were used to anoint the sick; 4) embalming—perfumed oil and ointment were used to prepare a body for burial.[3]

The approach

As the story unfolds, the sinful woman courageously comes where she is not wanted. She even presses in so closely that she can stand behind Jesus' out-stretched and unshod feet. It is unclear why she comes. Some commentators think she previously heard Jesus preach and had been convicted to repentance and new life. With love she comes to Simon's house to bestow her gift of expensive perfume. She begins weeping from the depth of her gratitude. Other commentators think this is the first time she has met Jesus, and being drawn into His presence convicts her. Because she weeps repentantly, it is clear that she is drawn to Jesus.

The woman wants to see Jesus, but as she looks, she comes right up close—to His feet, where convicted sinners find themselves—and His utter sinlessness undoes her. Standing so close to Him, she sees herself and releases the turbulent waters of her soul. Like the woman at the well, she is then given the water from which new life springs.

Intimate encounter

The woman forgets everyone except Jesus. She acts as though she were intimately alone with Him. Her actions are outside the bounds of appropriate public behavior. A Jewish girl binds up her hair on the day of her wedding, and it is an act of the "gravest immodesty" for a woman to appear in public with her hair unbound.[4] Her hair, her crowning glory, is to be enjoyed only by her husband. But perhaps the woman comes to Jesus as if He were the husband. Perhaps she is purposefully and publicly acknowledging to whom she belongs.

Like others...

Like the woman at the well meeting her True Husband, the sinful woman comes to her True Husband and joyfully discovers He knows her past and loves her still. As He did for the woman with the issue of blood, Jesus acknowledges her past and publicly restores her to a place in society. Like the healed leper who returns to Jesus, the woman comes to fall at His feet in worship. Like Rahab, who lifts her hand in service, the woman willingly raises her hand to serve. Like Rahab, who begs to be saved and is given a new chapter of life to live in peace, the woman silently begs to be saved and is given peace to live a new life chapter.

Unlike Simon...

Simon invites Jesus; the woman invites herself. Simon gives nothing to Jesus, even failing as a host to provide basic hospitable courtesies. The woman gives all she has, even willingly performing a servant's task. Simon reclines; the woman kneels. Simon places himself in front of Jesus near His head; the woman places herself behind Jesus at His feet. Simon waits to be served; the woman throws herself into His service. Simon is condescending; the woman is humble. Simon remains distant; the woman approaches. Simon doesn't approve of her touching Jesus; the woman wants to touch Jesus.

Simon thinks he is a religious man; the woman knows she is a sinner. Simon feels no need of forgiveness and does not love; the woman is forgiven and accepted and feels the need to respond with overwhelming love. Simon doubts Jesus' authority to forgive sins; the woman places her faith in Jesus and receives forgiveness.

Simon does not see through the eyes of Jesus; therefore, Simon thinks Jesus cannot see who the woman is. But Jesus knows who the Pharisee thinks Jesus is and who the Pharisee thinks the woman is. Simon sees the sin; Jesus sees the sinner. Simon sees her offenses; Jesus sees her need. Simon sees the magnitude of her depravity; Jesus sees the depth of her love.

Unlimited response

Like a music video, the woman acts out the love song of her heart. Gratitude wells up and spills over. Nothing is too good for Jesus, no service too great, no sacrifice too big. Jesus puts no limit on the amount of love you may give Him and gives no rules for your response to Him. Imagine perfect freedom to express yourself!

mining the message

1. List the actions of this woman as outlined in the passage. Then imagine the range of emotions she experienced. Identify what her emotions might have been from before she entered Simon's house to the end of the scene, when she heard Jesus say, "Your faith has saved you; go in peace."

----

draw your story

6

Draw a picture of the three main characters (Jesus, Simon, and the woman) around the table.

What is the position of the characters in relation to each other? Is Jesus in the center? Is this significant? What did the woman give to Jesus? Could you draw it? Are you able to discern the attitude of the characters by the posture you drew? Is someone else able to?

2. What reasons does Simon have to be upset about the actions of this woman? Why do you think Simon, as the host of the occasion, doesn't simply stop the action and send the woman out of his house?

3. Why do you think Jesus ignores the purification law that forbids anyone from touching or being touched by a prostitute? (Jesus is made ceremonially unclean by this woman's touch and is required to go through the purification ritual outlined in the Levitical law in order to enter the Temple for worship.)

4. What does Simon's unspoken question about Jesus reveal about his understanding of who Jesus is? about his relationship to Jesus? How do you think Simon feels when he realizes that Jesus knows what he is thinking in his heart?

5. How do you think Simon hears the parable Jesus tells? How does the woman hear it? How do the other guests hear it? Why does Jesus use a parable to make His point to Simon?

6. Jesus follows His parable with a public rebuke to Simon for his inhospitality. Why? Does this seem out of character for Jesus? Explain your answer.

7. Three hospitable customs were performed for a guest who entered an ancient Jewish home: 1) upon the guest's arrival, a host gives a kiss of peace, which marks respect for the guest; 2) a servant washes the guest's feet to remove the dust of the streets; 3) a few drops of perfume are poured on the guest upon arrival or when reclining at the table to eat. Sometimes the perfume is placed upon the beard, feet, and clothing.[5]

   If good manners dictate these courtesies for each guest, why do you think Simon does not do these for Jesus? What does this reveal about Simon?

8. Washing Jesus' feet was a sign of deep humility; it was the job of a slave. How do you think the woman feels when she realizes Jesus knows her heart?

9. With whom do you most identify in this story: Simon, the woman, the other guests? Why? Why didn't the storyteller finish the story about Simon? Do you think Simon becomes a believer? Why or why not?

Reflection story

How could she be so stupid? Using her own home… In her own marriage bed… Her children playing in the yard… Forgetting that her sister-in-law was dropping off the cousins for an afternoon of play. Stupid! Stupid! Stupid!

The entire ugly scene played over and over. The door opening… The startled look… The scramble to cover up… Her lover's rush from the house… Pleading with her sister-in-law: "Stop! Wait! Don't take the kids. I can explain."

She started to hyperventilate. How could anyone explain? The panic spread. She lay immobile on the tidied bed… waiting.

He didn't come home. She pulled herself together to call her sister-in-law about the kids. No answer. Will he stay away? Will he take the kids with him? Should she leave? Where could she go?

Clothes flew into the suitcase. All her instincts compelled her to run.

The car in the driveway jolted her. It was him… alone. What could she say?

Without fixing the smears of makeup staining her face, without straightening her clothes, she waited.

The door opened. He stood motionless, crushed.

Silence.

"Do you love him?"

"I thought so… but… it wasn't like… I can't…"

Silence.

"What do you want?"

"Is there any way… Can we…?"

Silence.

Then the torrent rained. "It was such a mistake. I don't know how I got so enmeshed. I knew all the time it was wrong. I thought of you, of us, of the kids. It was so stupid. I'm so ashamed. I'm so sorry. Can you ever forgive me? Is there any way we can begin again?"

His arms enveloped her. He waited until her sobbing stopped. He petted her hair and whispered, "It'll be OK. It'll be OK."

"How can you be so… so… sure?"

He lifted her face in both hands to meet his gaze. "Don't you get it? I love you. I always have. I always will. No matter what." His voice broke as he continued. "This can make our marriage stronger… if we both work at it. It will take time. It will be tough, but we can do it."

It was tough. But it did work. He never said another word about her headlong fall. But she never forgot it. When that terrible day played again in her memory, she didn't think about being caught, or her shame, or the humiliation. She thought about a man who loved her enough to forgive, about the blessings to their relationship that had come, and about the unbreakable bond between them. And she praised God… every day… joyfully.

Reflect

What does this story demonstrate about healing? about forgiveness?

Living the truth

Have your actions ever been misunderstood or criticized? How did you respond?

----

integrate

Simon needs to hear Jesus confirm that the woman is no longer the kind of woman Simon had known. Are you ready to extend forgiveness to others?
Leave the space below for a special assignment from the Bible study leader after you have viewed the DVD for Session 6, "Joy: An Expensive Perfume."

SCRIPTURE PROMISE

Praise be to God,
who has not
rejected my prayer
or withheld his
love from me!

PSALM 66:20

NOTES

[1] Kenneth L. Barker et al in *NIV Archaeological Study Bible* (Grand Rapids: Zondervan, 2005), p. 1599.

[2] Bruce B. Barton et al in *Luke, Life Application Bible Commentary* (Carol Stream: Tyndale House Publishers, 1997), p. 188.

[3] Barker, in *NIV Archaeological Study Bible,* p. 1746.

[4] William Barclay, *The Gospel of Luke,* p. 95.

[5] *Ibid.,* p. 93.

[6] E. Earle Ellis, *The Gospel of Luke, The New Century Bible Commentary* (Grand Rapids: Wm. B. Eerdmans Publishing Company, 1996), p. 122.

journal your journey

Men pay this woman to touch them with her hands, hair, lips; yet she gives her service—her ultimate gift—to Jesus for free as an act of worship. She lavishly anoints Him like a king by using the most expensive perfumed oil (the typical hospitality anointing is only a drop or two of olive oil).[6]

What is the most precious gift you can give Jesus? What should you be giving to Him that you've been giving elsewhere? Is anything holding you back from breaking the neck of your alabaster jar and spilling every drop on His feet? What is it, and what do you need to do about it, by God's grace?

Zelophehad's daughters
UNITED
WE STAND

OBJECTIVES

In this lesson you will

- Examine the story of the daughters of Zelophehad.

- Compare their actions and possible motives with those of Caleb and his daughter.

- Reflect on the meaning of receiving an inheritance.

- Identify issues around you that you believe need to be changed.

- Discover what you can do in your sphere of influence to bring about change.

ASSIGNMENT FOR THIS LESSON

1. Read the Scripture story.

2. Complete the worksheets for this lesson.

3. As you Journal Your Journey, talk to God about receiving your inheritance as His daughter.

Numbers 26:33 ✦ The Census

³³(Zelophehad son of Hepher had no sons; he had only daughters, whose names were Mahlah, Noah, Hoglah, Milcah, and Tirzah.)

Numbers 27:1-11 ✦ Zelophehad's Daughters

¹The daughters of Zelophehad son of Hepher, the son of Gilead, the son of Makir, the son of Manasseh, belonged to the clans of Manasseh son of Joseph. The names of the daughters were Mahlah, Noah, Hoglah, Milcah and Tirzah. They approached ²the entrance to the Tent of Meeting and stood before Moses, Eleazar the priest, the leaders and the whole assembly, and said, ³"Our father died in the desert. He was not among Korah's followers, who banded together against the Lord, but he died for his own sin and left no sons. ⁴Why should our father's name disappear from his clan because he had no son? Give us property among our father's relatives."

⁵So Moses brought their case before the Lord ⁶and the Lord said to him, ⁷"What Zelophehad's daughters are saying is right. You must certainly give them property as an inheritance among their father's relatives and turn their father's inheritance over to them.

⁸"Say to the Israelites, 'If a man dies and leaves no son, turn his inheritance over to his daughter. ⁹If he has no daughter, give his inheritance to his brothers. ¹⁰If he has no brothers, give his inheritance to his father's brothers. ¹¹If his father had no brothers, give his inheritance to the nearest relative in his clan, that he may possess it. This is to be a legal requirement for the Israelites, as the Lord commanded Moses.'"

Numbers 36:1-12 ✦ Inheritance of Zelophehad's Daughters

¹The family heads of the clan of Gilead son of Makir, the son of Manasseh, who were from the clans of the descendants of Joseph, came and spoke before Moses and the leaders, the heads of the Israelite families. ²They said, "When the Lord commanded my lord to give the land as an inheritance to the Israelites by lot, he ordered you to give the inheritance of our brother Zelophehad to his daughters. ³Now suppose they marry men from other Israelite tribes; then their inheritance will be taken from our ancestral inheritance and added to that of the tribe they marry into. And so part of the inheritance allotted to us will be taken away. ⁴When the Year of Jubilee for the Israelites comes, their inheritance will be added to that of the tribe into which they marry, and their property will be taken from the tribal inheritance of their forefathers."

⁵Then at the Lord's command Moses gave this order to the Israelites: "What the tribe of the descendants of Joseph is saying is right. ⁶This is what the Lord commands for Zelophehad's daughters: They may marry anyone they please as long as they marry within the tribal clan of their father. ⁷No inheritance in Israel is to pass from tribe to tribe, for every Israelite shall keep the tribal land inherited from his forefathers. ⁸Every daughter who inherits land in any Israelite tribe must marry someone in her father's tribal clan, so that every Israelite will possess the inheritance of his fathers. ⁹No inheritance may pass from tribe to tribe, for each Israelite tribe is to keep the land it inherits."

¹⁰So Zelophehad's daughters did as the Lord commanded Moses. ¹¹Zelophehad's

daughters—Mahlah, Tirzah, Hoglah, Milcah and Noah—married their cousins on their father's side. ¹²They married within the clans of the descendants of Manasseh son of Joseph, and their inheritance remained in their father's clan and tribe.

Joshua 17:1-6 ✦ Allotments for the Tribe of Manasseh

¹This was the allotment for the tribe of Manasseh as Joseph's firstborn, that is, for Makir, Manasseh's firstborn. Makir was the ancestor of the Gileadites, who had received Gilead and Bashan because the Makirites were great soldiers. ²So this allotment was for the rest of the people of Manasseh—the clans of Abiezer, Helek, Asriel, Shechem, Hepher and Shemida. These are the other male descendants of Manasseh son of Joseph by their clans.

³Now Zelophehad son of Hepher, the son of Gilead, the son of Makir, the son of Manasseh, had no sons but only daughters, whose names were Mahlah, Noah, Hoglah, Milcah and Tirzah. ⁴They went to Eleazar the priest, Joshua son of Nun, and the leaders and said, "The Lord commanded Moses to give us an inheritance among our brothers." So Joshua gave them an inheritance along with the brothers of their father, according to the Lord's command. ⁵Manasseh's share consisted of ten tracts of land besides Gilead and Bashan east of the Jordan, ⁶because the daughters of the tribe of Manasseh received an inheritance among the sons. The land of Gilead belonged to the rest of the descendants of Manasseh.

seeking through study

Inheritance laws

"Inheritance laws in the ancient Near East played a critical role in preserving a family line and perpetuating its land holdings. Wealth and social standing were tied to landed property, and rules of kinship regulated the land's division. Customary law held that only sons had the right to inherit, and the firstborn son received a double share of the family estate."[1] For the firstborn to receive a double portion, the estate was divided into thirds; he received two thirds, and all other sons divided the remaining third between them (Deuteronomy 21:15-17). "Since the land belonged to the Lord (Leviticus 25:23-28), the Jews couldn't divide it or dispose of it as they pleased."[2]

Traditionally, sons inherited land. Daughters inherited a dowry as portable property, such as servants, household vessels, and jewelry.

Census taking

Soon after the Exodus, Moses took the first census (recorded at the beginning of the book of Numbers), which numbered the men who were able to fight as soldiers. Just before going into Canaan about 40 years later, Moses took the second census (recorded at the end of the book of Numbers), which numbered the men who would receive an inheritance.

The challenge

To hear the court cases and hand down decisions, Moses, Eleazar the priest (son of Aaron), and the princes of the 12 tribes convened as a jury and assembled at the door of the tabernacle compound, which enabled Moses to arise easily and approach God to determine His will for any specific request or situation.[3]

Implicit in the challenge brought by the daughters of Zelophehad is the suggestion that God's own decrees given through Moses may have overlooked an important point. When the daughters bring their concern to Moses, the result is what some commentators describe as "progressive legislation" for circumstances as needed. (These changes in law were confined to civil affairs; the slightest change was inadmissible in laws relating to worship or the maintenance of religion.)[4]

Modeling for the future

Just as the daughters of Zelophehad united in a request, so their tribe (Manasseh) joined with their brother tribe (Ephraim) in the land of Canaan to request their inheritance. Joshua gave them the forested northern hill country and said, "Clear it, and its farthest limits will be yours; though the Canaanites have iron chariots and though they are strong, you can drive them out" (Joshua 17:18). Like Jesus who didn't stop the woman from anointing His feet, Joshua put no limits on the territory they could claim.

"Some of the tribes gladly accepted their inheritance and went to work making it 'home,' some complained about the land they were given, and some went out and conquered more territory. 'According to your faith be it unto you' (Matthew 9:29)."[5]

mining the message

1. Write a story title (or news headline) for each of the three petitioning scenes, with a subheading if needed.

✍ draw your story

7

Draw a picture of one of the scenes of the five women bringing their petition.
(Turn the page sideways if needed.)

How do you draw an intangible thing, such as inheritance, or an idea, such as justice?

2. How would the census prevent possible future problems in regard to the amount of land distributed to each tribe? Why would the men who were numbered receive an inheritance? What was the purpose of taking the second census (Numbers 26:52-56)?

----

3. To whom do the five daughters take their request? Why is this significant? What is unusual about their request to receive an allotment of land?

----

4. What does Moses do to prepare a response to their petition? How is this procedure the same or different from other unusual situations he is called upon to judge? (See Leviticus 24:10-16, blasphemer; Numbers 9:8, nonobservers of Passover; Numbers 15:32-36, Sabbathbreaker.)

----

5. How do Moses' actions protect this highly unusual decision that favors women? How does this decision set a precedent for future outside-the-box challenges?

----

6. Who has a problem with the decision to give land to Zelophehad's daughters (Numbers 36:1-12)? What are the reasons? Do you think the concerns are justifiable? Why or why not?

7. What does Moses do to respond to the objections? Do you think this second solution was fair to all parties concerned? Why or why not?

- -

- -

- -

- -

8. Identify three steps Moses prescribes for the daughters to follow. Do they accomplish this?

- -

- -

- -

- -

9. What is different in regard to Zelophehad's daughters bringing their request a second time to a new leader (Joshua 17:1-6)?

- -

- -

- -

- -

10. How are Israeli women in future decades and centuries affected by the actions of these five women? Do you think this would have happened if Zelophehad's daughters had not been united? Why or why not?

- -

- -

- -

- -

Reflection story

JoDee read the words in her local newspaper one more time. Nearly 50 percent of the homeless people in her city were children under the age of 10.

That did it! She could not sit idly by another minute and do nothing about homelessness in her town. Five phone calls later, six women sat around JoDee's kitchen table.

"This problem is so huge. Where can we start?"

They talked and talked and talked—then made a list of questions to answer:

Where do mothers with children find food and shelter?

Do homeless children receive schooling?

Which agencies and churches are helping homeless families?

Which ones are doing the best job?

What are homeless families' needs?

How much does the city spend per homeless child?

They divided the questions and set a date one week later to meet again with answers.

It had taken persuasion for JoDee's "Blessing Bunch" to get their large institutional church to open up to homeless families one week each quarter. Church and community volunteers helped each time. Some helped the families do their laundry in the washer and dryer in the church kitchen. Some hauled beds from the warehouse downtown. Some picked up food from the food bank and grocery store collection sites. Some fixed breakfast and supper each day. Kids from the academy tutored the children each evening and took them to the school gym for recreation.

They had talked to agencies, raised money, organized volunteers. And it was making a difference. *Their* children weren't sleeping in cars or cardboard boxes anymore.

JoDee helped the Sabbath school primary class carry their bundles to the cars waiting outside. Her group would deliver Christmas to one of four of their "homeless" families this year, families now in permanent housing. JoDee couldn't tell who was more excited, the primary kids or their parents—the drive to the house, the excitement when the family saw the Christmas tree on top of one car, the kids in the family helping the primary kids empty four cars full of gifts and food, the tears streaming down the cheeks of the mother as she stood waving goodbye.

JoDee had started with five friends. Now dozens of people were making a difference.

Reflect

Identify injustices or conditions that you would like to see changed. How could working in concert with other women impact these situations?

Living the truth

The daughters of Zelophehad weren't the only claimant party to file for an inheritance. A few years after the fall of Jericho, Caleb, the courageous comrade scout of Joshua, reminded him of the Lord's promise of an inheritance (Joshua 14:6-15). Later, Caleb's daughter Acsah petitioned for an inheritance. She asked her husband to apply to her father for a field, and then she herself requested springs of water to irrigate it (Joshua 15:18, 19).

When Caleb made his request, for what did it set a precedent? Do you think Caleb's request made a difference in how Joshua continued to work? Why do you think Acsah made her requests? What difference does it make for the future of our descendants if we do not speak up? How does this lesson apply to you?

integrate

Think about different causes or issues that arouse your emotions. What prevents you from taking action to make a difference in your future and the future of others? Leave the space below for a special assignment from the Bible study leader after you have viewed the presentation for Session 7, "United We Stand."

NOTES

[1] Walter C. Kaiser, Jr. and Duane Garrett in *NIV Archaelogical Study Bible* (Grand Rapids: Zondervan, 2005), p. 250.

[2] Warren W. Wiersbe, *Be Counted: Living a Life That Counts for God, An Old Testament Study—Numbers* (Colorado Springs: David C. Cook Publishing, 1996), p. 122.

[3] Francis D. Nichol, ed., *The Seventh-day Adventist Bible Commentary* (Hagerstown: Review and Herald Publishing Association, 1978), vol. 1, p. 927.

[4] Robert Jamieson, A. R. Fausset, and David Brown, *Commentary Critical and Explanatory on the Whole Bible* (Grand Rapids: Zondervan Publishing, 1871), p. 120. Note on Numbers 36:5-12.

[5] Wiersbe, p. 120.

> *Whom have I in heaven but you?*
> *And earth has nothing I desire besides you.*
> *My flesh and my heart may fail,*
> *But God is the strength of my heart*
> *And my portion forever.*

PSALM 73:25, 26

The land of Canaan is a metaphor for the Promised Land, where God dwells in peace and rests with His people forever. Everyone is an heir of God (see Galatians 3:26-29). What does it mean *to inherit* your portion? What is your *portion*?

The power of words
OFF WITH HIS HEAD!

OBJECTIVES

In this lesson you will

- Compare the actions of Herod with those of Pilate.
- Contrast the words of Herodias with those of Pilate's wife.
- Identify ways women exert their influence on others.
- Recognize the power of words for both good and evil.

ASSIGNMENT FOR THIS LESSON

1. Read the Scripture story.
2. Complete the worksheets for this lesson.
3. As you Journal Your Journey, talk to God about the dynamics driving your words.

Mark 6:14-29 ✦ John the Baptist Beheaded

[14]King Herod heard about this, for Jesus' name had become well known. Some were saying, "John the Baptist has been raised from the dead, and that is why miraculous powers are at work in him."

[15]Others said, "He is Elijah."

And still others claimed, "He is a prophet, like one of the prophets of long ago."

[16]But when Herod heard this, he said, "John, the man I beheaded, has been raised from the dead!"

[17]For Herod himself had given orders to have John arrested, and he had him bound and put in prison. He did this because of Herodias, his brother Philip's wife, whom he had married. [18]For John had been saying to Herod, "It is not lawful for you to have your brother's wife." [19]So Herodias nursed a grudge against John and wanted to kill him. But she was not able to, [20]because Herod feared John and protected him, knowing him to be a righteous and holy man. When Herod heard John, he was greatly puzzled; yet he liked to listen to him.

[21]Finally the opportune time came. On his birthday Herod gave a banquet for his high officials and military commanders and the leading men of Galilee. [22]When the daughter of Herodias came in and danced, she pleased Herod and his dinner guests.

The king said to the girl, "Ask me for anything you want, and I'll give it to you." [23]And he promised her with an oath, "Whatever you ask I will give you, up to half my kingdom."

[24]She went out and said to her mother, "What shall I ask for?"

"The head of John the Baptist," she answered.

[25]At once the girl hurried in to the king with the request: "I want you to give me right now the head of John the Baptist on a platter."

[26]The king was greatly distressed, but because of his oaths and his dinner guests, he did not want to refuse her. [27]So he immediately sent an executioner with orders to bring John's head. The man went, beheaded John in the prison, [28]and brought back his head on a platter. He presented it to the girl, and she gave it to her mother. [29]On hearing of this, John's disciples came and took his body and laid it in a tomb.

Matthew 27:11-26 ✦ Jesus Before Pilate

[11]Meanwhile Jesus stood before the governor, and the governor asked him, "Are you the king of the Jews?"

"Yes, it is as you say," Jesus replied.

[12]When he was accused by the chief priests and the elders, he gave no answer. [13]Then Pilate asked him, "Don't you hear the testimony they are bringing against you?" [14]But Jesus made no reply, not even to a single charge—to the great amazement of the governor.

[15]Now it was the governor's custom at the Feast to release a prisoner chosen by the crowd. [16]At that time they had a notorious prisoner, called Barabbas. [17]So when the crowd had gathered, Pilate asked them, "Which one do you want me to release to you: Barabbas, or Jesus who is called Christ?" [18]For he knew it was out of envy that they had handed Jesus over to him.

[19]While Pilate was sitting on the judge's seat, his wife sent him this message: "Don't have anything to do with that innocent man, for I have suffered a great deal today in a dream because of him."

[20]But the chief priests and the elders persuaded the crowd to ask for Barabbas and to have Jesus executed.

[21]"Which of the two do you want me to release to you?" asked the governor.

"Barabbas," they answered.

[22]"What shall I do, then, with Jesus who is called Christ?" Pilate asked.

They all answered, "Crucify him!"

[23]"Why? What crime has he committed?" asked Pilate.

But they shouted all the louder, "Crucify him!"

[24]When Pilate saw that he was getting nowhere, but that instead an uproar was starting, he took water and washed his hands in front of the crowd. "I am innocent of this man's blood," he said. "It is your responsibility!"

[25]All the people answered, "Let his blood be on us and on our children!"

[26]Then he released Barabbas to them. But he had Jesus flogged, and handed him over to be crucified.

seeking through study

Both sides of the family tree—from the same branch

To understand the characters in the story of John's beheading (and their relationships to each other), we need to explore their family tree and find out more than is recorded in the Bible. The writings of the Jewish historian Josephus carefully chronicle their family history. Scholars agree that there are few families in history with the convoluted relationships surrounding Herod the Great.

The Herod referred to in Mark 6 is Herod Antipas, son of Herod the Great. Herodias is a granddaughter of Herod the Great.

Cast of characters

Herod the Great: King of Judea and Idumea, Samaria, Galilee and Peraea, and the Northeast (Iturea and Traconitis). He is appointed by the Romans as tetarch in 41 B.C. and allowed to reign as king from 37 B.C. to A.D. 4. Herod is king in Jerusalem when Jesus is born in Bethlehem. The visit from the Wise Men adds fuel to his blatantly blazing desire to protect his throne. He is notoriously remembered as the Herod who massacred baby boys in Bethlehem. But he also murders many other people, including his own sons and their mothers. A common Jewish saying was "It is safer to be Herod's pig than Herod's son."[1]

Herod the Great is a foreigner who marries Mariamne, a Jewish descendant of the Hasmonean Judas Maccabaeus. Her family is considered to have been the most influential of Jewish political leaders of the time. No doubt they would have become Jewish aristocracy had they been able to gain the throne from Rome. Herod kills most of the Hasmoneans, including his wife Mariamne and their sons.

Aristobulus: Son of Herod the Great and Mariamne the Hasmonean. Aristobulus names his daughter Herodias, the feminine version of his murderous father's name. His son Herod Agrippa is appointed tetarch after Herod Antipas is sent into exile by the Romans. Aristobulus and his mother are also murdered by Herod the Great.

Herodias: Daughter of Aristobulus. She marries her father's half-brother Philip I and bears his daughter Salome. She leaves Philip I to marry her brother-in-law, Herod Antipas. Herodias is a granddaughter of the Jewish Mariamne.

Herod Philip I: Son of Herod the Great and Mariamne the Boethusian, daughter of a priest. He is the half brother of Antipas. He does not reign over any territory, but lives in luxury in Rome. He marries Herodias, daughter of Aristobulus, his half brother. Philip I sires a daughter with Herodias named Salome. Therefore, Philip's daughter is also his great-niece.

Herod Antipas: Son of Herod the Great and Malthace the Samaritan. He is ruler over one fourth his father's kingdom and is officially the tetrarch of Galilee and Perea, a lower level of Roman civic leadership than king, but he styles himself King Herod (after his father's name).

He visits his half brother Philip I in Rome and seduces his sister-in-law Herodias to leave her husband and return to Palestine to marry him, even though he must yet divorce his first wife, the daughter of King Aretas of Nabatea (Arabia). Therefore, Antipas' second wife is his sister-in-law and also his niece.

Salome: Daughter of Philip I and Herodias. She dances for Antipas, her stepfather and great uncle. Perhaps it is the work of a courtesan is to dance for such celebrations as Antipas' birthday feast. But Bible scholars note that a "solo dance" before a group of Eastern men was the art of professional prostitutes, and would be a highly unusual performance for a princess of the royal bloodline.[2] Salome marries her great uncle Philip II. Therefore, Salome's husband is the half brother of both her father and her stepfather.

John the Baptist: Prophet in the Judean wilderness who calls people to repent of their sins and be baptized. He is cousin to Jesus of Nazareth. John the Baptist speaks out about the Herod-Herodias relationship, which is adulterous and incestuous.

The setting

John the Baptist is incarcerated in the dungeon of the fortress of Machaerus on an elevated ridge overlooking the east side of the Dead Sea. Bible scholar William Barclay calls Machaerus "one of the loneliest and grimmest and most unassailable fortresses in the world."[3] Apparently, it is also the location of the infamous birthday party.

The plot

Herod Antipas has seduced his sister-in-law Herodias. They have left their spouses to live together and are seeking divorces. According to Jewish law, a brother of a deceased husband may marry his sister-in-law if she needs to be provided with an heir. However, in this case, the woman is not a widow—her husband is still very much alive. And Herodias, the granddaughter of a king, is a wealthy woman who has the means to support herself and her daughter. Yet to silence forever the voice of the man who has dared to denounce their sinful actions, Herodias commands Salome to ask for his head on a platter.

Pilate's wife

Although the Bible doesn't mention the name of Pilate's wife or give any background information about her, she is identified in apocryphal writings as Claudia Procula, a granddaughter of the emperor Augustus, and was a convert to Judaism. Her interest in the Jewish religion may have been an additional reason, besides her dream, for her sharp interest in Jesus.

mining the message

1. List the characters in the Mark 6:14-29 story and write an epitaph for their tombstones.

----

draw your story

Draw a picture from either story.

Do you identify with any of the characters in the story you drew? Why?

2. Characterize Herodias. What is she like? What similarities do you see between her and Jezebel (2 Kings 9:3-37)?

---

3. What reasons does Herod Antipas have to arrest John? What reasons does Antipas have to protect John while keeping him in prison?

---

4. Antipas gives the order for John to be executed even though he knows John is a righteous and holy man. Why does he do this? What does this tell us about Antipas?

---

5. Are Salome and Antipas pawns of Herodias (Mark 6:21)? Explain your answer.

---

6. Who is most responsible for John the Baptist's death? Rank each of the following from most responsible to least responsible: party guests, Herod Antipas, Herodias, Salome, the executioner.

(most responsible)

(least responsible)

7. In the second Scripture story (Matthew 27:11-26), Pilate has Jesus flogged and then crucifies Him, even though he knows that Jesus is innocent. He does this in spite of the message his wife sends warning him to have nothing to do with Jesus (verse 19). What are his reasons for doing this? What does this tell us about Pilate?

-----

8. How do you think Pilate's wife felt when her words went unheeded?

-----

9. Compare the motives of Herod, Herodias, and Pilate. What is the compelling motivation driving all three?

Reflection story

The first time Annie left Richard she went straight home to her mother. Annie had surrendered her house key when she married, so she stood on the doorstep holding a suitcase, embarrassed to be ringing the doorbell.

Her mother opened the door, took one look at Annie, and said, "Go back home to your husband. He's a good man, and he loves you. Whatever is going on between you two, work it out."

Annie had returned home humiliated. She didn't want to work it out; she wanted the marriage to be over.

Life had gotten so complicated. Little annoyances had escalated into major fights. The only shoulder to cry on belonged to Mike, her coworker. For months Annie imagined ways to end her marriage, but none of them would leave her as the "innocent" party. She expected her friends and family to condemn divorce for any reason save adultery, and Richard was faithful to her. She knew that, and so did everyone else. At work Mike pressed her to take the next step in their relationship. His impatience annoyed her. She could wait.

Then Annie thought of something that would work. Like a lightning strike, the chain of events slashed through their lives: the accusation that Richard was sexually abusing their preschool daughter, his arrest, the caseworker's interview, the courtroom scene, Richard in jail, the divorce papers signed and sealed.

Annie's lawyer asked the judge to give Richard the maximum sentence. Annie looked so magnanimous pleading for the minimum. And her mother—she fluttered about Annie like a moth to a flame.

Annie's triumph felt incredible.

Reflect

Think about the power of words and what that power can accomplish. Why do you think words have such power?

Living the truth

Imagine a scale of selfishness with Herodias on one end as "most self-absorbed" and Pilate's wife at the other end as "most concerned about another's welfare." Where on the scale would you place yourself? Why?

SELF-ABSORBED   CONCERNED FOR OTHERS

| 1 | 2 | 3 | 4 | 5 | 6 | 7 | 8 | 9 | 10 |

integrate

Are you listening to the Word of God? Are you choosing to say the right words, or are you speaking the wrong words?

Save the space below for a special assignment from the Bible study leader after you have watched the presentation for Session 8, "Off With His Head."

NOTES

[1] William Barclay, *The Gospel of Mark, The Daily Study Bible Series,* revised edition (Philadelphia: Westminster Press, 1975), p. 149.

[2] *Ibid.,* p. 152.

[3] *Ibid.,* p. 149.

journal your journey

Do not let any unwholesome talk come out of your mouths,
but only what is helpful for building others up according to their needs,
that it may benefit those who listen.
EPHESIANS 4:29

What insights can you gather from this verse? What motivates your words? How can you take responsibility for your words? How would your life be different if you put the words of the text into practice in your life?

Eve

EAT TODAY FOR TOMORROW WE DIE

OBJECTIVES

In this lesson you will

- Analyze the words of God, Eve, and the serpent.

- Identify consequences of the Fall for those involved.

- Develop an awareness of deceptive strategies.

- Discover ways to protect yourself against deception.

ASSIGNMENT FOR THIS LESSON

1. Read the Scripture story.

2. Complete the worksheets for this lesson.

3. As you Journal Your Journey, talk to God about where He wants you to focus your attention.

worship in the word

Genesis 3:1-24 ✦ The Fall of Man

¹Now the serpent was more crafty than any of the wild animals the LORD God had made. He said to the woman, "Did God really say, 'You must not eat from any tree in the garden'?"

²The woman said to the serpent, "We may eat fruit from the trees in the garden, ³but God did say, 'You must not eat fruit from the tree that is in the middle of the garden, and you must not touch it, or you will die.'"

⁴"You will not surely die," the serpent said to the woman. ⁵"For God knows that when you eat of it your eyes will be opened, and you will be like God, knowing good and evil."

⁶When the woman saw that the fruit of the tree was good for food and pleasing to the eye, and also desirable for gaining wisdom, she took some and ate it. She also gave some to her husband, who was with her, and he ate it. ⁷Then the eyes of both of them were opened, and they realized they were naked; so they sewed fig leaves together and made coverings for themselves.

⁸Then the man and his wife heard the sound of the LORD God as he was walking in the garden in the cool of the day, and they hid from the LORD God among the trees of the garden. ⁹But the LORD God called to the man, "Where are you?"

¹⁰He answered, "I heard you in the garden, and I was afraid because I was naked; so I hid."

¹¹And he said, "Who told you that you were naked? Have you eaten from the tree that I commanded you not to eat from?"

¹²The man said, "The woman you put here with me—she gave me some fruit from the tree, and I ate it."

¹³Then the LORD God said to the woman, "What is this you have done?"

The woman said, "The serpent deceived me, and I ate."

¹⁴So the LORD God said to the serpent, "Because you have done this,

"Cursed are you above all the livestock
    and all the wild animals!
You will crawl on your belly
    and you will eat dust
    all the days of your life.
¹⁵And I will put enmity
    between you and the woman,
    and between your offspring and hers;
he will crush your head,
    and you will strike his heel."

¹⁶To the woman he said,

"I will greatly increase your pains in childbearing;
    with pain you will give birth to children.
Your desire will be for your husband,
    and he will rule over you."

¹⁷To Adam he said, "Because you listened to your wife and ate from the tree about which I commanded you, 'You must not eat of it,'

"Cursed is the ground because of you;
    through painful toil you will eat of it
    all the days of your life.

18It will produce thorns and thistles for you,
  and you will eat the plants of the field.
19By the sweat of your brow
  you will eat your food
  until you return to the ground,
    since from it you were taken;
  for dust you are
    and to dust you will return."

20Adam named his wife Eve, because she would become the mother of all the living.

21The LORD God made garments of skin for Adam and his wife and clothed them. 22And the LORD God said, "The man has now become like one of us, knowing good and evil. He must not be allowed to reach out his hand and take also from the tree of life and eat, and live forever." 23So the LORD God banished him from the Garden of Eden to work the ground from which he had been taken. 24After he drove the man out, he placed on the east side of the Garden of Eden cherubim and a flaming sword flashing back and forth to guard the way to the tree of life.

seeking through study

Where is God?

We hear about the serpent—he is "more crafty than any of the wild animals"—even before we hear him speak. His craftiness is evidenced by being able to strip God of His intimate divine name (Yahweh signifies a personal Creator-God) without appearing to be the embodiment of an evil creature spouting bold-faced lies. He gracefully glides near and his tone is friendly and open, even incredulous or conspiratorial, as if taking the woman into his confidence. He flicks his tongue, and out flies the question still being asked today. "Did God really say…?"

By referring to the woman's Creator simply as God (perhaps god), the serpent leaves an opening of doubt over Yahweh's supremacy. Without her cognizance of the subtlety in this sleight-of-hand maneuver, Yahweh is demoted and placed on the shelf, equal to other trophy gods. Confusion over which god is in question occurs when we speak of the Lord God no differently than any other god. He becomes like them: arbitrary, selfish, and cloaked in secrecy. Yet the serpent conceals his own intent even while accusing the Lord of the same thing.

Turning aside

One pastor-scholar describes the dynamics of the encounter this way: "In the moment the woman turns aside to see the serpent, she loses sight of Yahweh." When not focused on God, she focuses on her desires. When not looking to God, she desires to become as God.

Questions are asked about God's word. "Did God really say…?" Doubts are raised regarding the fairness of God's word. "If He really loved you, He would be more generous. He's holding out on you!" Outright denial is spoken against God's word regarding something so desirable. "You will not die. You will become like the gods."[1]

"The serpent's temptation to the woman was that she should doubt God's word. It seemed in context so unreasonable that God should have made this one small prohibition."[2] Don't you want to know what you don't know? Suddenly the gap between God and the serpent narrows greatly. Now only small steps remain to be taken from believing God's word, to denying God's word, to believing Satan's lies.

A covenant God

Yahweh reappears in the story when He actively seeks out the hiding couple. It is the Lord God who walks, calls out, asks questions, pronounces judgment, covenants a promise, makes garments, clothes the man and woman, banishes them from access to the Tree of Life, and drives them out of the garden.

No longer the guardian of the garden, the man needs a protector and provider. The couple is promised restoration and healing for their broken relationship with Yahweh. The True Gardener will provide the Seed who will become their True Guardian.

Living while dying

Ironically, the serpent was partly correct when he proclaimed, "You shall not surely die." Rather than dying instantly, Eve lived for a long time and became the mother of all living persons on the earth. Rather than giving up and continuing to hide, Adam believed the promise with regard to the woman's seed and showed this faith through the name he chose for his wife.[3] "Eve" sounds like the word for life and living.

Every baby is the potential Seed. Not only does bearing children fulfill the destiny set forth by God, who commands, "Be fruitful and multiply" (Genesis 1:28, King James Version), but it provides God with every opportunity possible to fulfill His covenant. Babies are precious and desired; however, the woman must now suffer every time she bears children. In traditional societies a woman longed to be the mother of a large family.[4] Yet the more children she wanted, the more pregnancies and painful labors she had to undergo.

mining the message

1. Why would Eve respond to a talking animal and not simply leave the scene? What does this reveal about her?

2. Which portions of the serpent's statements are true and which are false? Why is mixing truth with lies an effective strategy?

---

3. The Hebrew word recorded in Genesis 2:17 is definite: "You will surely die." The word recorded in Eve's response is translated "lest ye die" (King James Version), implying only a possibility that they "might" die. Compare Eve's other responses to the serpent with the words God actually spoke to Adam. What changes does Eve make, and why is it significant that Eve makes these changes?

LORD GOD GENESIS 2:16, 17; 3:22	SERPENT GENESIS 3:1, 4, 5	EVE GENESIS 3:2, 3
You are free to eat from any tree in the garden;	Did God really say, "You must not eat from any tree in the garden"?	We may eat fruit from the trees in the garden,
But you must not eat from the tree of the knowledge of good and evil,		But God did say, "You must not eat fruit from the tree that is in the middle of the garden,
For when you eat of it, you will surely die.	You will not surely die.	And you must not touch it, or you will die" [lest ye die].
The man has now become like one of us, knowing good and evil.	For God knows that when you eat of it your eyes will be opened, and you will become like God, knowing good and evil.	

---

4. Would Eve have been so gullible if the tempter had looked evil or spoken in a frightening way? Why do you think the tempter did not present himself as an angel of light, as he did to Jesus in the wilderness?

----

5. Identify three reasons Eve ate the forbidden fruit (Genesis 3:6). Do you think these are feminine dynamics? Explain your answer. Why do you think Adam ate the fruit? Are his reasons masculine? Explain your answer.

----

6. List the consequences of the Fall for all four players: Adam, Eve, the serpent, God. Which consequence do you think would be the hardest for Eve to bear and why?

----

7. How do you think each of these—Adam, Eve, and the serpent—heard the words recorded in Genesis 3:15? Where is the good news in this story?

8. It's easy to look at Eve and think *Wow! Was she ever stupid! If I'd been there, I would never have fallen for that stuff!* Imagine yourself in her place. In what ways are you like Eve? How are you different?

---

draw your story

Draw a picture of the story.

How do you represent concepts such as doubt and fear, disobedience and rebellion? Did you find symbolism in literal objects or spoken words?

Reflection story

When the doctor walked into her hospital room, Lori didn't bother drying her tears. She looked soberly at him. "The floor nurse called me," he said. "I guess she's been checking on you every ten minutes." Lori hadn't noticed.

"I know this is hard on you," he continued.

How does he know? Does he have a child with fetal alcohol syndrome?

After a pained minute of silence, he asked: "Is there anything I can do for you?"

Lori shook her head. He threw around a few platitudes. "You're not the first person to have to deal with this, you know. There are wonderful agencies to help you. This will work out. You'll be OK." She looked at him as if he had dropped in from another planet. After a quick squeeze on her hand, he left.

The next day it was the hospital chaplain, the head nurse, her roommate, even a janitor chimed in. *What do they know? This life sentence isn't theirs.*

Josh had mercifully stayed away. Could she ever forgive him for upbraiding her in the delivery room?

How stupid can a person be? she sobbed. There was no escape from the consequences of a few drinks. *My baby, my baby,* she cried. *What have I done?*

She could still see Josh's face when the doctor told them. "There seems to be a little problem here. We'll need to get a specialist in." That bomb blast had silenced every person in the delivery room. The only noise was the baby crying pitifully.

She hadn't wanted to hold him. A La Leche League mother had "dropped in" to help her start breast feeding. Lori watched, amazed, as she tenderly coaxed the baby and cooed to him as if he were normal. "Every baby's such a precious gift. Don't you think?" She looked Lori in the eyes. Lori dropped her gaze. The woman coaxed her, too, placing Lori's hands on the baby's head and bottom.

How strange that little bundle felt, so light, so fragile. A new instinct crept into her as she gazed at the tiny face with its familiar shape. She pulled him close and cuddled him. She would take this baby home. She would love him like no other. She would protect him. God help anyone who hurt this baby.

Lori and Josh jumped and shouted and hugged each other and yelled, "Go, Joey, go!" He had become a favorite at the Special Olympics. Their doctor had been right about one thing: there were agencies and wonderful people with compassion for kids like their Joseph. It had been tough, especially those first years, but they had banded together like a platoon on patrol. The sweetness of his temperament, the genuineness of his affection, had wrapped around their hearts.

Joey broke the ribbon across the finish line. "God is good," Lori said.

"All the time," Josh added, squeezing her hand.

Reflect

Are you living with consequences of wrong choices you have made—shame, guilt, regret, broken relationships, failure, loss? Where in the story of Eve is there hope for you?

Living the truth

How do we know from this story that God does not want us to live with guilt and regret even though we must live with the consequences of our wrong choices?

----

integrate

One theologian outlines the serpent's strategy as presenting enticements. Notice the subtle steps.

- "I can give you something you need and want."
- "You can have it now and enjoy it."
- "There won't be any painful consequences."

Through this method the serpent exaggerated the divine instruction, caricatured God's character, and hooked Eve to believe the open denial and bold-faced lie.[5]

Which of these strategies seem the most compelling to you? Why?

Leave the space below for a special assignment from the Bible study leader after you have viewed the presentation for Session 9, "Eat Today for Tomorrow We Die."

NOTES

[1] Warren W. Wiersbe, *Be Basic: Believing the Simple Truth of God's Word, An Old Testament Study—Genesis 1-11* (Colorado Springs: Victor Books, 1998), pp. 59, 60.

[2] David Atkinson, *The Message of Genesis 1-11, The Dawn of Creation, The Bible Speaks Today, Old Testatment Series* (Downers Grove: InterVarsity Press, 1990), p. 84.

[3] Francis D. Nichol, ed., *The Seventh-day Adventist Bible Commentary,* (Hagerstown: Review and Herald Publishing Association, 1978), vol. 1, p. 235.

[4] Gordon J. Wenhem, *Word Biblical Commentary, Genesis 1-15* (Waco: Word Books, 1987), vol. 1, p. 89.

[5] Arthur J. Ferch, *In the Beginning: Genesis* (Hagerstown: Review and Herald Publishing Association, 1985), p. 42.

journal your journey

9

Is there a big picture that you're not able to see because you're focusing on the small stuff? What in Eve's story and in God's response can help you change your focus?

Joseph
DREAMS FULFILLED

OBJECTIVES

In this lesson you will

- Examine the life of Joseph while he was in Egypt.

- Compare his dreams as a youth to his life as an adult.

- Discover the key to Joseph's success in an alien land and the fulfillment of his dreams.

- Ponder your own times of trouble and whether you remained faithful to God.

- Reflect on the forgiveness issues addressed in the life of Joseph and in your own life.

ASSIGNMENT FOR THIS LESSON

1. Read Joseph's story in Genesis 39-41.

2. Imagine yourself in the palace on the day Joseph was brought before Pharaoh.

3. As you journal, compare Joseph's character and circumstances with your own. Take time to reflect and talk to God about your circumstances.

4. Try to work on this lesson each day in the coming week.

5. Think about what you desire God to do in your life.

Genesis 39:1-20 ✦ Joseph and Potiphar's Wife

[1] Now Joseph had been taken down to Egypt. Potiphar, an Egyptian who was one of Pharaoh's officials, the captain of the guard, bought him from the Ishmaelites who had taken him there.

[2] The LORD was with Joseph and he prospered, and he lived in the house of his Egyptian master. [3] When his master saw that the LORD was with him and that the LORD gave him success in everything he did, [4] Joseph found favor in his eyes and became his attendant. Potiphar put him in charge of his household, and he entrusted to his care everything he owned. [5] From the time he put him in charge of his household and of all that he owned, the LORD blessed the household of the Egyptian because of Joseph. The blessing of the LORD was on everything Potiphar had, both in the house and in the field. [6] So he left in Joseph's care everything he had; with Joseph in charge, he did not concern himself with anything except the food he ate.

Now Joseph was well-built and handsome, [7] and after a while his master's wife took notice of Joseph and said, "Come to bed with me!"

[8] But he refused. "With me in charge," he told her, "my master does not concern himself with anything in the house; everything he owns he has entrusted to my care. [9] No one is greater in this house than I am. My master has withheld nothing from me except you, because you are his wife. How then could I do such a wicked thing and sin against God?" [10] And though she spoke to Joseph day after day, he refused to go to bed with her or even be with her.

[11] One day he went into the house to attend to his duties, and none of the household servants was inside. [12] She caught him by his cloak and said, "Come to bed with me!" But he left his cloak in her hand and ran out of the house.

[13] When she saw that he had left his cloak in her hand and had run out of the house, [14] she called her household servants. "Look," she said to them, "this Hebrew has been brought to us to make sport of us! He came in here to sleep with me, but I screamed. [15] When he heard me scream for help, he left his cloak beside me and ran out of the house."

[16] She kept his cloak beside her until his master came home. [17] Then she told him this story: "That Hebrew slave you brought us came to me to make sport of me. [18] But as soon as I screamed for help, he left his cloak beside me and ran out of the house."

Joseph Sent to Prison

[19] When his master heard the story his wife told him, saying, "This is how your slave treated me," he burned with anger. [20] Joseph's master took him and put him in prison, the place where the king's prisoners were confined.

Genesis 41:8-40 ✦ Pharaoh's Dreams

[8] In the morning his mind was troubled, so he sent for all the magicians and wise men of Egypt. Pharaoh told them his dreams, but no one could interpret them for him.

[9] Then the chief cupbearer said to Pharaoh, "Today I am reminded of my shortcomings. [10] Pharaoh was once angry with his servants, and he imprisoned me and the chief baker in the house of the captain of the guard. [11] Each of us had a dream the same night, and each dream had a meaning of its own. [12] Now a young Hebrew was there with us, a servant of the captain of the guard. We told him our dreams, and he

interpreted them for us, giving each man the interpretation of his dream. [13]And things turned out exactly as he interpreted them to us: I was restored to my position, and the other man was hanged."

[14]So Pharaoh sent for Joseph, and he was quickly brought from the dungeon. When he had shaved and changed his clothes, he came before Pharaoh.

[15]Pharaoh said to Joseph, "I had a dream, and no one can interpret it. But I have heard it said of you that when you hear a dream you can interpret it."

[16]"I cannot do it," Joseph replied to Pharaoh, "but God will give Pharaoh the answer he desires."

[17]Then Pharaoh said to Joseph, "In my dream I was standing on the bank of the Nile, [18]when out of the river there came up seven cows, fat and sleek, and they grazed among the reeds. [19]After them, seven other cows came up—scrawny and very ugly and lean. I had never seen such ugly cows in all the land of Egypt. [20]The lean, ugly cows ate up the seven fat cows that came up first. [21]But even after they ate them, no one could tell that they had done so; they looked just as ugly as before. Then I woke up.

[22]"In my dreams I also saw seven heads of grain, full and good, growing on a single stalk. [23]After them, seven other heads sprouted—withered and thin and scorched by the east wind. [24]The thin heads of grain swallowed up the seven good heads. I told this to the magicians, but none could explain it to me."

[25]Then Joseph said to Pharaoh, "The dreams of Pharaoh are one and the same. God has revealed to Pharaoh what he is about to do. [26]The seven good cows are seven years, and the seven good heads of grain are seven years; it is one and the same dream. [27]The seven lean, ugly cows that came up afterward are seven years, and so are the seven worthless heads of grain scorched by the east wind: They are seven years of famine.

[28]"It is just as I said to Pharaoh: God has shown Pharaoh what he is about to do. [29]Seven years of great abundance are coming throughout the land of Egypt, [30]but seven years of famine will follow them. Then all the abundance in Egypt will be forgotten, and the famine will ravage the land. [31]The abundance in the land will not be remembered, because the famine that follows it will be so severe. [32]The reason the dream was given to Pharaoh in two forms is that the matter has been firmly decided by God, and God will do it soon.

[33]"And now let Pharaoh look for a discerning and wise man and put him in charge of the land of Egypt. [34]Let Pharaoh appoint commissioners over the land to take a fifth of the harvest of Egypt during the seven years of abundance. [35]They should collect all the food of these good years that are coming and store up the grain under the authority of Pharaoh, to be kept in the cities for food. [36]This food should be held in reserve for the country, to be used during the seven years of famine that will come upon Egypt, so that the country may not be ruined by the famine."

[37]The plan seemed good to Pharaoh and to all his officials. [38]So Pharaoh asked them, "Can we find anyone like this man, one in whom is the spirit of God?"

[39]Then Pharaoh said to Joseph, "Since God has made all this known to you, there is no one so discerning and wise as you. [40]You shall be in charge of my palace, and all my people are to submit to your orders. Only with respect to the throne will I be greater than you."

Genesis 45:1-8 ✦ Joseph Makes Himself Known

[1]Then Joseph could no longer control himself before all his attendants, and he cried out, "Have everyone leave my presence!" So there was no one with Joseph when he made himself known to his brothers. [2]And he wept so loudly that the Egyptians heard him, and Pharaoh's household heard about it.

³Joseph said to his brothers, "I am Joseph! Is my father still living?" But his brothers were not able to answer him, because they were terrified at his presence.

⁴Then Joseph said to his brothers, "Come close to me." When they had done so, he said, "I am your brother Joseph, the one you sold into Egypt! ⁵And now, do not be distressed and do not be angry with yourselves for selling me here, because it was to save lives that God sent me ahead of you. ⁶For two years now there has been famine in the land, and for the next five years there will not be plowing and reaping. ⁷But God sent me ahead of you to preserve for you a remnant on earth and to save your lives by a great deliverance.

⁸"So then, it was not you who sent me here, but God. He made me father to Pharaoh, lord of his entire household and ruler of all Egypt."

seeking through study

A Man of God

Have you ever wondered how Hollywood would make a movie today about the life of Joseph? It has all the elements of a grand movie epic: adventure, betrayal, dramatic rise from prisoner to prime minister, and the all-important sex scenes where the handsome hero gets seduced by his boss's lonely, neglected wife. Except for one thing: the hero consistently rebuffs the beautiful seductress and even flees from her presence. How boring—by Hollywood standards. But from the Bible we know that God's standards and the world's standards are at odds.

The story of Joseph is the story of a man who dreamed as a 17-year-old of being used by God in a position of leadership and authority, and who held on to that dream his entire life. It was a God-given dream,[1] one that required the dreamer to be true to God despite betrayal, loneliness in a foreign land, temptation, and bitter disappointment. The fact that Joseph was able to be true to his dreams—and to God—in spite of repeated setbacks and very real temptations is what makes this a great epic by Christian standards.

Joseph has been called the most Christlike character in the Old Testament. In many ways he seems too good to be true. How can we, as 21st century women, relate to someone so nearly perfect? What is God trying to tell us through Joseph's story?

Betrayed

Joseph's lengthy story is found in Genesis 37 and 39-50. Joseph's father petted and pampered him, resulting in his brothers hating him and eventually finding a way to get rid of him (see Genesis 37:12-36). Suddenly Joseph went from being an indulged favored son to being a slave in a strange land—alone, abused, abandoned.

According to one Bible commentator, "the name of God does not appear, and his hand is at present only dimly seen among the wicked designs, deeds, and devices of these unnatural brothers. Nevertheless, his counsel of mercy standeth sure, and fixed is his purpose to bring salvation to the whole race of man."[2]

It is said that a person's character is revealed in the fire of adversity. When

Joseph was sold to Potiphar, a captain in the king's guard, his sterling character and work ethic did not go unnoticed. Potiphar came to rely more and more on Joseph, and he was eventually put in charge of running the captain's household. God's blessing in Joseph's life was evident even to an unbeliever.

Tempted

Joseph was in his mid-20s when he was propositioned by Potiphar's wife—in the very prime of a man's sexuality. Though the seductress made advances to Joseph "day after day," and there was little fear of being caught by her husband with him away on Pharaoh's business, Joseph's high principles gave him the strength to resist. Considering how lonely he must have been in a foreign country without anyone dear and familiar to him, it is a remarkable testimony to his strong sense of loyalty and responsibility,[3] not just to his God, but also to his master. Despite the circumstances, Joseph remained faithful to both.

A woman scorned

Joseph soon discovered that there were dreadful consequences for maintaining his high principles. "Her [Potiphar's wife] disappointment now provokes her to falsehood as the means of concealment and revenge."[4] A few short hours after fleeing her bedroom he found himself in the dungeon, even though Potiphar believed more strongly in Joseph's integrity than in his wife's story.[5] Somehow, doing the right thing turned out horribly wrong.

For a while Joseph seems to have been treated quite severely in prison (see Psalm 105:18), but his integrity and faithfulness under deplorable prison conditions resulted in the same rise in responsibility that had occurred in Potiphar's house. In a short time Joseph was assistant to the prison warden and involved in the day-to-day running of the prison.[6]

Shut out again

Genesis 40 details Joseph's time in prison and his correctly interpreting the dreams of the baker and cupbearer, as well as his profound disappointment when the cupbearer failed to remember him to Pharaoh. As a year passed after the cupbearer left prison, then another year, the now 30-year-old Joseph must have wondered what chance his dreams had at this point. Where was the God who gave him those dreams? Why was He silent? Joseph must have cried out, "Are You there? Do You hear me?"

We discover the answer to that question when Pharaoh has his dream (Genesis 41). When none of his magicians and wise men could interpret the dream, the cupbearer suddenly remembered Joseph and told Pharaoh about the dreams that he and the baker each had while in prison, which Joseph correctly interpreted.

Pharaoh immediately called for Joseph to be brought to him. And *now* we see why God allowed the two-year delay. Simply stated, Pharaoh had not needed a dream interpreter until now. If the cupbearer had told him about Joseph earlier, Pharaoh would not have been interested. God's timing was perfect!

As Joseph began to interpret the king's dream, "he was so filled with the Spirit of God that he was endowed with wisdom and discernment and was therefore completely *sure* about the message of the dreams. This certainty gave him the *courage* to tell the king both the 'good news and the bad news' contained in the dreams. Most important of all, it gave him the *confidence* to propose God's plan of deliverance from the terrible predictions of the dreams."[7]

"He immediately enters upon his office. The fulfillment of the dream here commences.... Two sons were born to Joseph during the seven years of plenty. He tenderly and intensely remembered his father's house. But he is grateful to God, who builds him a home, with all its soothing joys even in the land of exile. His heart again responds to long-untasted joys.

"He bears in mind those early dreams of his childhood. All his subsequent experience has confirmed him in the belief that they will one day be fulfilled.... He leaves all in the hand of God, and awaits in anxious but silent hope the days when he will see his father and his brothers."[8]

The Big Picture

Follow Joseph's meeting with his brothers and the astonishing account of the forgiveness he offered them. Three times he broke down and wept loudly over them (Genesis 42:24; 43:30, 31; 45:1, 2), not only because forgiveness was difficult, but also because he feared they could not forgive themselves.[9] Incredibly, Joseph offered comfort to his betrayers (Genesis 45:4-8).

"He [Joseph]... plainly refers to the fact of their having sold him. He points out that this was overruled by God to save lives and hence that it was not they, but God, who had mercifully sent him to Egypt to preserve all their lives.... Having touched very slightly on their transgression, and endeavored to divert their thoughts to the wonderful providence of God displayed in the whole affair, he lastly preoccupies their minds with the duty and necessity of bringing down their father and all their families to dwell in Egypt.... He breaks through all distance, and falls upon Benjamin's neck and kisses him, and all his brothers; after which their hearts are soothed, and they speak freely with him."[10]

Note that Joseph did not downplay what his brothers had done to him. In Genesis 45:4 he tells them that he is the brother they sold into Egypt. Again in Genesis 50:20 Joseph is blunt with his brothers: "You intended to harm me..." But he doesn't stop there. The rest of the verse says: "...but God intended it for good to accomplish what is now being done, the saving of many lives."

Joseph was able to see The Big Picture. He didn't dwell on the evil of his brothers' betrayal and the horrors he had experienced during the long years in slavery. Joseph's life centered not on himself but on the will of God and the importance of God's purposes being accomplished. The twenty years he had spent in Egypt before being reunited with his family did not seem like a waste of time, as he now saw how God had used his experiences to save his family. Interestingly, Joseph's brothers' treachery proved to be the means of their own salvation.

Dreams realized

Though it took thirteen difficult years, Joseph's youthful dream of being used by God in extraordinary ways came to fruition. According to David Seamands, "there is no biblical story which better illustrates the overarching providence of God in our lives than that of Joseph.... Even in the most unlikely incidents in Joseph's life, God was at work, making them turn out for His purposes."[11]

mining the message

1. According to Genesis 39:3, why does Potiphar entrust a slave with everything he had?

2. Why did Potiphar's wife notice Joseph?

Joseph evidently inherited his good looks from his mother, Rachel, who is described in Genesis 29:17 as "lovely in form, and beautiful," the same language used to describe Joseph in Genesis 39:6.

3. Analyze Joseph's situation with Potiphar's wife. There were advantages and risks to Joseph on each side of this temptation. Identify the advantages and risks of giving in and of refusing Potiphar's wife.

4. What do the two reasons Joseph gave for refusing Potiphar's wife tell us about him? Do you think this temptation was easy or difficult for Joseph? Explain your answer.

5. What do you think would have happened to the inner person of Joseph if he had yielded to Potiphar's wife's advances? Could he have maintained his integrity? Would he have been able to pretend that he was a man of virtue?

6. Read Psalm 105:17-19, which describes Joseph's physical suffering. In addition to his physical suffering, in how many other ways did Joseph suffer because of his integrity?

7. How do we know that Joseph didn't succumb to a "victim" mentality? Describe a victim mentality.

8. What do you think was the secret of Joseph's success? Is there an area in your life in which relying on God will empower your integrity?

9. Someone has said that holding on to anger and resentment is like taking poison and waiting for the other person to die. How difficult is it for you to forgive those who have wronged you? How do you apply Jesus' words in the Lord's Prayer to your life: "Forgive us our debts, as we also have forgiven our debtors" (Matthew 6:12)—or, in other versions, "Forgive us our trespasses, as we forgive those who trespass against us"?

10. In The Big Picture of your life, can you see the hand of God? What part has adversity played—or is playing—in your life?

Draw a picture of the scene in Genesis 45:1-8. Remember that Joseph looked like an Egyptian prime minister, while his brothers were nomadic Hebrew shepherds.

Are the brothers happy or sad, gathered close together or standing in a line? How does your picture make you feel? Can you see that God has been with Joseph throughout his journey?

Reflection story

Lana and the other accountants in the firm had burned the midnight hours preparing for the board of directors meeting. Two days and counting. Fatigue plagued her. What a relief it would be to see that neat stack of printed reports waiting, ready.

Mr. Thornton, her immediate superior, walked to her cubicle and tossed a thick packet onto Lana's desk. "I want you to cook the books on this, then bury it." How strange his lips looked—like elastic—as he whispered each syllable. Thornton's eyes darted from cubicle to cubicle.

Lana's thoughts flashed back to her first week on the job two years earlier. How could she have been so blessed as to land a position with this company? Her "dream job," she announced to anyone who asked.

In the months that had followed, hard work and rave reviews from Thornton had secured her future as an "up-and-comer." Now a fear crawled up her back. She felt trapped by her dependence upon that fat monthly paycheck.

"How, in this economy, will I pay my bills if I lose this job?"

It's not that big a deal. Just do it and keep your mouth shut.

"What will I be asked to do next time?"

Everybody does it. He'll just ask someone else if you say no.

"I won't do anything illegal, Mr. Thornton," Lana said quietly.

Thornton positioned himself on her desk and zeroed his gaze. "You'll do what you're told if you want to continue working here."

The seconds moved like a tsunami as Thornton waited. "I understand," she said as she pushed away from her computer station and stood facing him. After he left, Lana picked up the thick manila envelope as if it contained anthrax.

At home Lana felt surprised at her energy level as she spent the night hours studying the financial report. Finally she figured out how she could hide Thornton's mess. She wondered if anyone besides Thornton knew about this.

A hard knot in the pit of her stomach sent a wave of nausea to her throat.

What should she do? Whom could she go to: Thornton's immediate superior; the CEO? Was this a setup for her to take the fall?

Lana got to work early and looked busy as she waited for Thornton to arrive. When he finally settled at his desk with coffee mug in hand, she walked quickly to his office door. With her hand on the knob, she closed her eyes for a long second. With a confidence she didn't feel, she walked briskly to his desk, laid the package in front of him, and said, "I won't do anything with this."

"What the —," he cursed. "Are you too stupid to figure it out?"

"No, Mr. Thornton. I'm too smart."

His jaw dropped, but he quickly recovered. "Don't expect to get another job…"

She interrupted him: "My desk is already cleared."

Reflect

Have you ever been asked to compromise your principles? Were you able to resist? If you did or if you did not, how did it affect your self-respect?

Living the truth

Imagine yourself trapped in your circumstances and waiting for God to set you free to fulfill His plan for your life. Will you be free at the beginning of the outside of the maze or beginning at the center and finding your way out? Begin your journey at the outside or in the center. At the place where God commences His plan for you, draw a little YOU.

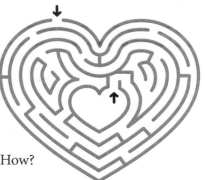

Will you wait for God to work out His plan for your journey? How?

----

integrate

Think about all the disappointments Joseph experienced from the time he was sold into slavery until he was made prime minister of Egypt. What about your own disappointments? How have they changed you?

Leave the space provided below for a special assignment from the Bible study leader after you have viewed the presentation for Session 10, "Dreams Fulfilled."

SCRIPTURE PROMISE

*And we know that
in all things
God works for the good
of those who love him,
who have been
called according to
his purpose.*
ROMANS 8:28

Instructions for

Journal your journey

According to Oswald Chambers, "The circumstances of a saint's [a child of God] life are ordained of God. In the life of a saint there is no such thing as chance. God by His providence brings you into circumstances that you can't understand at all, but the Spirit of God understands. God brings you to places, among people, and into certain conditions to accomplish a definite purpose through the intercession of the Spirit in you."[12]

For your journaling time this week, reflect on this passage in relation to Joseph's life and to your own. Have you cooperated with God as Joseph did? Have you had to wait? How might your life have been different if you had allowed God to use you more? What can you do in the future to be used by God in accomplishing His divine purposes?

NOTES

[1] Francis D. Nichol, ed., *The Seventh-day Adventist Bible Commentary,* (Hagerstown: Review and Herald Publishing Association, 1978), vol. 1, p. 429.

[2] James G. Murphy, *Barnes' Notes "A Commentary on The Book of Genesis"* (Grand Rapids: Baker Books, reprinted 1998) p. 445.

[3] David A. Seamands, *Living With Your Dreams* (Wheaton: Victor Books, 1990), p. 57.

[4] Murphy, p. 453.

[5] *The Seventh-day Adventist Bible Commentary,* vol. 1, p. 440.

[6] Seamands, p. 81.

[7] *Ibid.,* p. 95.

[8] Murphy, pp. 464, 465.

[9] Seamands, p. 140.

[10] Murphy, p. 484.

[11] Seamands, p. 148.

[12] Oswald Chambers, *My Utmost for His Highest, An Updated Edition in Today's Language,* edited by James G. Reimann (Grand Rapids: Discovery House Publishers, 1992), November 7.

journal your journey

10

11

Sarah

AN OLD LADY HAS THE LAST LAUGH

"She who laughs last laughs best"

OBJECTIVES

In this lesson you will

- Examine the story of the promise and birth of Isaac.

- Compare and contrast Abraham's and Sarah's laughs.

- Discern the true meaning and source of joy.

- Reflect on what you have learned from these lessons.

- Discover how you can experience joy in your life every day.

ASSIGNMENT FOR THIS LESSON

1. Read Genesis 18:1-15; 21:1-7.

2. Underline key words or phrases; then write the main point of these passages in a phrase or sentence.

3. Complete the worksheets for this lesson.

4. Examine your life to determine where you need to grow.

5. As you Journal Your Journey, talk to God about your feelings regarding the gift of joy He is offering you.

worship in the word

Genesis 18:1-15 ✦ The Three Visitors

[1]The LORD appeared to Abraham near the great trees of Mamre while he was sitting at the entrance to his tent in the heat of the day. [2]Abraham looked up and saw three men standing nearby. When he saw them, he hurried from the entrance of his tent to meet them and bowed low to the ground.

[3]He said, "If I have found favor in your eyes, my lord, do not pass your servant by. [4]Let a little water be brought, and then you may all wash your feet and rest under this tree. [5]Let me get you something to eat, so you can be refreshed and then go on your way—now that you have come to your servant."

"Very well," they answered, "do as you say."

[6]So Abraham hurried into the tent to Sarah. "Quick," he said, "get three seahs of fine flour and knead it and bake some bread."

[7]Then he ran to the herd and selected a choice, tender calf and gave it to a servant, who hurried to prepare it. [8]He then brought some curds and milk and the calf that had been prepared, and set these before them. While they ate, he stood near them under a tree.

[9]"Where is your wife Sarah?" they asked him.

"There, in the tent," he said.

[10]Then the LORD said, "I will surely return to you about this time next year, and Sarah your wife will have a son."

Now Sarah was listening at the entrance to the tent, which was behind him. [11]Abraham and Sarah were already old and well advanced in years, and Sarah was past the age of childbearing. [12] So Sarah laughed to herself as she thought, "After I am worn out and my master is old, will I now have this pleasure?"

[13]Then the LORD said to Abraham, "Why did Sarah laugh and say, 'Will I really have a child, now that I am old?' [14]Is anything too hard for the LORD? I will return to you at the appointed time next year and Sarah will have a son." [15]Sarah was afraid, so she lied and said, "I did not laugh."

But he said, "Yes, you did laugh."

Genesis 21:1-7 ✦ The Birth of Isaac

[1]Now the LORD was gracious to Sarah as he had said, and the LORD did for Sarah what he had promised. [2]Sarah became pregnant and bore a son to Abraham in his old age, at the very time God had promised him. [3]Abraham gave the name Isaac to the son Sarah bore him. [4]When his son Isaac was eight days old, Abraham circumcised him, as God commanded him. [5]Abraham was a hundred years old when his son Isaac was born to him.

[6]Sarah said, "God has brought me laughter, and everyone who hears about this will laugh with me." [7]And she added, "Who would have said to Abraham that Sarah would nurse children? Yet I have borne him a son in his old age."

seeking through study 11

Two special visits

During his first ten years of living in Canaan, Abraham apparently enjoyed several visits from God. But there is no record of God talking to him in the thirteen years after Ishmael's birth. Abraham may have wondered during those silent years if God would ever reveal Himself again. But when He appears to Abraham in Genesis 17, it is for a specific reason—to declare that Sarah will be the mother of the chosen heir.

At His next visit (Genesis 18:10-14) God chooses a different way of appearing to Abraham, and this time to Sarah also. He comes in human form with two companions. Abraham greets them and entertains them lavishly. Then, as they linger after the meal, God asks where Sarah is.

It would have been out of keeping with Oriental custom for visitors of a Bedouin sheik to inquire about the host's wife, especially using her given name. If Abraham had any previous suspicions that his visitors were more than human, this would likely have confirmed them.[1]

Abraham was convinced by God's prior visit that Sarah would bear the promised child. It seems probable, therefore, that this visit is more for Sarah's benefit than Abraham's. This is the only time the Bible records Sarah's involvement in a divine conversation. Perhaps, through this very special visit, God was preparing her for the supreme experience of her life.

Why did you laugh?

People laugh for many reasons. Sometimes we laugh because something is truly funny. Often, though, we laugh because we're nervous or embarrassed.

Some people laugh when they're scared or sad, or when they're lying or being sarcastic. Sometimes people laugh to cover their pain. We often laugh when things are ironic, unexpected, or downright crazy. Occasionally we say, "I don't know whether to laugh or cry!"

Sarah had known about the promise of an heir for nearly 25 years. But that she, in her old age, should become a mother seemed beyond belief. In Genesis 18:12 Sarah laughs in bitterness and incredulity at this impossible notion.

Is anything too hard?

Sarah's name means "princess." And indeed, this strikingly beautiful woman had a "kingdom" over which to rule. The book *Patriarchs and Prophets* indicates there were more than a thousand people in Abraham's household.[2] But whatever satisfaction Sarah derived from her status did not make up for being barren.

Barrenness was quite possibly the worst thing that could happen to a woman in Sarah's culture. Sarah could probably have endured leaving her home and traveling around living in tents if she could have experienced the pleasure of producing for Abraham the promised offspring and becoming the mother of a great nation. But that had not happened. Instead, she had been forced to live year after year with the stigma of her barrenness.

At this point in the story Sarah is old. She has no child, and is well past the age for bearing children. There is seemingly nothing left in life for her.

"Where human wisdom and strength fail, and where nature, enfeebled, lacks ability to act, there God still has full sway and brings things to pass according to His own divine will. In fact, He often permits circumstances to reach an impasse so that human impotence may stand forth in striking contrast to His omnipotence."[3]

The miracle

The name of God, El-Shaddai (translated "God Almighty"), is found only in the books of Genesis and Job. The use of the term in this story underscores the point that nothing, however difficult it seems to humans, is impossible for God.[4]

God had planned from the beginning that the birth of Isaac would be a token of the fulfillment of a larger promise—the coming of the Messiah.[5] Isaac's parents may have laughed in doubt at first, but they would surely rejoice when the event occurred. And his name (meaning "he laughs") would be a constant reminder that their faith had become reality.

At the appointed time, the miracle child was born. And no doubt Sarah laughed. Her first recorded laugh reflected cynicism and unbelief. But her second laugh was filled with joy. The fulfillment of God's promises always brings joy.

The gift of joy

In her book *Joy* Celeste perrino Walker states that joy is a gift from God that gives us the emotional fuel we need for our journey. Joy is not the giddy emotion of happiness that changes depending on such things as the weather, what activity we are doing, or how much money we have in the bank. Neither is joy a "happy pill" that makes us oblivious to our surroundings. But when we have it inside, it takes us beyond the present and focuses our minds on the future. Joy is deep, constant and abiding. "It keeps our mind-set steadfastly where it ought to be—on God's divine plan."[6]

Joy comes from trusting God—from believing that He has your best interest in mind and is working things out for your good. Joy comes from realizing that nothing can touch you that God hasn't allowed for some reason. Jesus gives us joy so that we won't let our lives be ruled by circumstances.

Joy is receiving from God His plan and believing He will fulfill it, even if it seems illogical or unexpected. One of the main points of Kent A. Hansen's book *Cleansing Fire, Healing Streams* (Pacific Press Publishing Association, 2007) is that the surest sign of the presence of God in one's life is living joyfully regardless of circumstances.

"Faith in God's love and overruling providence lightens the burdens of anxiety and care. It fills the heart with joy and contentment in the highest or lowliest lot."[7] We may at times laugh or cry because our journeys are difficult or take unexpected twists. But ultimately we can rest secure in the knowledge that we don't have to understand everything or even try to figure it all out.

Genesis 18:25 says, "Will not the Judge of all the earth do right?" We can trust God to make everything right at the journey's end. And we can trust Him to stay beside us every step of the way.

1. How many times previously had God promised Abraham a son? What is different about this time?

   ----

2. God obviously knew where Sarah was, so why did He ask? At what point do you think Abraham and Sarah realized that this visitor was God?

   ----

3. Why did Sarah laugh? Compare and contrast Sarah's laughter to Abraham's laughter in Genesis 17:17. Why do you think God rebuked Sarah for laughing but not Abraham? Do you think God was angry with Sarah for laughing?

   ----

4. Why do you think Sarah denied laughing?

   ----

5. How old were Abraham and Sarah when Isaac was born? Why is their age significant? How long had they waited for this child?

   ----

6. What does the name *Isaac* mean? Why do you think God chose this name?

   ----

7. Contrast Sarah's laughter in Genesis 18 with that in Genesis 21. Why does Sarah laugh now?

   ----

8. Perhaps you have heard the saying (attributed to Ella Wheeler Wilcox): Laugh, and the world laughs with you; weep, and you weep alone. What does Sarah's comment that "everyone… will laugh with me" reveal about her feelings through the long years of barrenness?

_____

_____

draw your story

To which of the characters in this story do you best relate? Draw yourself into a scene from their lives.

Reflection story

Her family marveled at her. None of them had expected Ruthie to be the one to take Dad in. They all knew about Dad and her. They had always known about Dad and her. Everyone, that is, except... Mom. Now Mom was gone. Too late to ask her why. *Why didn't you save me? Why didn't you stop him?*

Blind, Ruthie thought. *Mom's marvelous blind eye!*

None of them had wanted Dad, so like a stray puppy he had settled into Ruthie's house. She chuckled to herself because none of them knew why.

Fifty years had worked in her favor. Now he was in her control.

She planned carefully, patiently squirreling away a few pills each week for the job. Every day as she gave him his meds, she imagined what it would be like to do it that last time. To watch his eyes when he realized what she had done—realized the scales between them were balanced at last.

Then it came. The day. His regular pills rested in plastic mini-cups on the tray. The powder from 50 additional pills was dissolved in the applesauce he used to swallow his meds. She walked to his bedside and smiled down at him. But his eyes looked different.

Oh, no. Have I waited too long?

"Sit down, sugar," he said softly.

Ruthie sat.

Each word came with effort. She leaned close. "What I did to you was SO wrong. I know it hurt you—deeply. Not a day goes by, not one, that I don't wish I could go back and stop myself. I'm so sorry. I don't deserve you.

"I'm dying. I can't ask you to forgive me. I just want you to be OK, to be happy in spite of me."

She held his hand as that last breath slowly poured out. Then she closed his eyes and called the family to come.

Ruthie had been right. That day did change things. But not as she had expected. Never in a hundred lifetimes could she have dreamed up this ending... rather, this beginning.

She laughed, loud and long and deep.

Reflect

Have you or a loved one ever experienced a pain so deep that it robbed you of your hopes, your dreams, your joy in life? Can you relate to someone who is going through this kind of grief?

Living the truth

Think about the significance of Genesis 18:14. Where in your life is God asking you, "Is there anything too hard for Me?"

When Sarah tried to "help" God by encouraging Abraham to have a child with Hagar, things did not go well. For Sarah, having what she thought she wanted became the thorn in her flesh. Can you recall a time you tried to "help" God? What did you learn from the experience?

----

integrate

Nehemiah 8:10 assures us, "the joy of the Lord is your strength." Couple that text with our series theme text, "My presence will go with you. I'll see the journey to the end" (Exodus 33:14, *Message*). How do these texts assure you that you can have joy in your journey, despite your circumstances?

Leave the space provided below for a special assignment from the Bible Study leader after you have viewed the DVD for Session 11, "An Old Lady Has the Last Laugh."

SCRIPTURE PROMISE

Blessed are you who weep now,
> *for you will laugh.*

LUKE 6:21

Turn to page 134 to

journal your journey

NOTES

[1] Francis D. Nichol, ed., *The Seventh-day Adventist Bible Commentary,* (Hagerstown: Review and Herald Publishing Association, 1978), vol. 1, p. 327.

[2] Ellen G. White, *Patriarchs and Prophets* (Mountain View: Pacific Press Publishing Association, 1890), p. 141.

[3] *The Seventh-day Adventist Bible Commentary,* vol. 1, p. 328.

[4] *Ibid.,* pp. 320, 321.

[5] *Ibid.,* p. 344.

[6] Celeste perrino Walker, *Joy* (Hagerstown: Review and Herald Publishing Association, 2005), p. 15.

[7] White, p. 600.

Journal your Journey

Do you really believe that God is with you and that He can be trusted to work everything out in your life? If so, what is holding you back from experiencing the gift of joy He is offering you? If you have received the gift of joy, how are you sharing it with others?

NAMES, NOTES, & NUMBERS

my presence will go with you. I'll see the journey to the end.

EXODUS 33:14, *Message*